EARLY
IN THE
MORNING

EARLY
IN THE
MORNING

DEVOTIONS FOR EARLY RISERS

WOODROW M. KROLL

LOIZEAUX
Neptune, New Jersey

Originally Published in Two Volumes
First Combined Edition
May 1994

A publication of LOIZEAUX BROTHERS, Inc.
A nonprofit organization devoted to the Lord's work
and to the spread of His truth

Library of Congress Cataloging-in-Publication Data

Kroll, Woodrow Michael, 1944-
Early in the morning / Woodrow M. Kroll. — 1st combined ed.
"Originally published in two volumes"—T.p. verso.
ISBN 0-87213-476-8
1. Meditations.   I. Title.
BV4832.2.K75   1994
242—dc20   94-15183

PRINTED IN THE UNITED STATES OF AMERICA

10   9   8   7   6   5   4   3   2   1

Dedicated to
all my students
who have had to rise

EARLY IN THE MORNING
to attend my classes

Contents

Preface

Although there are twenty-four hours in each day, some of those hours are more glorious than others. By far the freshest hours of the day for me, and the most productive, are those that precede the glistening rays of the morning sun. It is then that I meet the Commander-in-Chief and get my marching orders for the day. If I fail to meet Him first, I usually fail to meet Him entirely.

An unknown poet expressed it this way:

A moment in the morning—a moment, if no more—
Is better than an hour when the trying day is o'er.

'Tis the gentle dew from heaven, the manna for the day;
If you fail to gather early—alas! It melts away.

God does things "early in the morning." Each of these devotional stories centers on a biblical event that occurred at the dawning of the day. It is my prayer that by meditating "early in the morning" on these early morning events each of us will walk more closely with the Lord throughout the day. After all, if we do not begin the day with Him, how can we spend the day with Him?

Prayer Line

MORNING SCRIPTURE   Psalm 59:1-17
MORNING VERSE   Psalm 59:16
But I will sing of Thy power; yea, I will sing aloud of Thy mercy in the morning: for Thou hast been my defense and refuge in the day of my trouble.

Although he had never heard the words, David knew well the lesson of James 5:16, "The effectual fervent prayer of a righteous man availeth much." Constantly being pursued by Saul and his men, David knew he must consistently pray to God for deliverance. He needed an open line to Heaven, a prayer line, and he needed to use that line frequently.

David begins Psalm 59 with a prayer: "Deliver me from mine enemies, O my God: defend me from them that rise up against me." Deliverance from enemies and oppressors is the almost constant cry of David (cf. Psalms 22:20; 25:20; 31:1-2, 15; 35:17; 40:13; 43:1; etc.). Here, however, David is still crying out to God and praising Him for deliverance from Saul's many attempts to assassinate him. He notes that Saul's men "lie in wait" for his soul and "run and prepare themselves without my fault" (Psalm 59:3). Saul had sent his emissaries to David's house "to watch him and to slay him in the morning" (1 Samuel 19:11). Time and time again David was close enough to Saul's men to hear them making noises like a dog. Still, time and time again, God delivered him from the wrath of Saul and his men.

The psalmist is confident of deliverance from his oppressors and declares, "But Thou, O LORD, shalt laugh at them." God miraculously arranged for David's malicious enemies to be made the objects of ridicule. For example, Saul's men had been made fools of by Michal, David's wife (cf. 1 Samuel 19: 12). With a twinkle of confidence shining through, David exclaims, "The God of my mercy shall prevent me." He knew that continued deliverance was but a prayer away.

Confident of his deliverance, the psalmist resolved, "I will sing of Thy power...of Thy mercy in the morning" (Psalm 59:16). While the wicked howl, the righteous sing. It is simply the nature of each. Throughout the night David would be pursued by the wicked men of Saul, but by morning's first light, he would be found singing praises unto God for His power and mercy. The psalmist rightly joins these two divine attributes together. Take away God's strength and He cannot protect us. Take away His mercy and He will not protect us. The two go hand in hand and become ours each time we stretch the prayer line to Heaven.

There is a woman in Kansas who promised many people she would remember them daily in prayer. Because she was a busy woman, washing and ironing daily throughout the week, she came to realize that it would be difficult to fulfill her prayer commitments to her friends. Then one day as she looked out the window she saw clothes drying on the line and an idea came to her. She strung a cord across one corner of her kitchen and hung cards on it with the names of those for whom she had promised to intercede. Now, while she does her ironing, she prays for those whose names are on the cards. The secret to her prayer life is the consistency with which she remembers those for whom she has promised to pray. She literally has a "prayer line" in her kitchen.

Although David had no kitchen, and no cord stretched across it, he too had a prayer line to God. He consistently referred to the throne of grace all the difficulties that he encountered. He aroused himself to pray every morning because he knew that God had been his defense and refuge throughout the night.

What a joy it is to greet the morning by greeting God in prayer. Though the dogs of distress howl all night, with the first light of morning comes the song of power and mercy. Don't neglect a consistent, early morning prayer time with the Lord. It will make a positive day for you.

MORNING HYMN
> *Teach me to pray, Lord, teach me to pray;*
> *This is my heartcry, day unto day;*
> *I long to know Thy will and Thy way;*
> *Teach me to pray, Lord, teach me to pray.*

Thinking of Others

MORNING SCRIPTURE   Genesis 19:15-29
MORNING VERSE   Genesis 19:27
*And Abraham got up early in the morning to the place where he
stood before the LORD.*

S elfishness is innate to man's being. Human philosophy
says, "Look out for number one for if you don't, no one
else will." The question of the first murderer, "Am I my
brother's keeper?" is still being asked in society today. This is
indeed unfortunate. When we live self-centered lives we are
denied the joy of delighting in others.

Abraham was a man little given to such selfishness. When
he and nephew Lot came to a parting of the ways, Abraham
gave his kin first pick of the land. Looking eastward on the fertile plain of the Jordan, Lot fell prey to temptation and chose
the valley thick with vegetation. Abraham then withdrew to
the oaks of Mamre, near Hebron, in the center of the south hill
country. Willing to obey the stern inward call of duty, Abraham
quietly received the less desirable terrain.

The picturesque valley of the lower Jordan was dotted with
five "cities of the plain." They were Sodom, Gomorrah, Admah,
Zeboiim, and Bela, which was later renamed Zoar. Sodom, the
chief city of this pentapolis, was so wicked that a particularly
abnormal sin bears its name. Here the worldly Lot chose to settle
and even become prominent. The men of this city were especially wicked and sinned exceedingly before the Lord. How it
must have grieved the genuinely pious Abraham to see his
nephew choose these surroundings.

In the course of time three angelic guests stopped at the
door of Abraham's tent in Mamre. Abraham greeted them hos-
pitably and made ready a feast. As the men prepared to leave,
Abraham accompanied them a short distance toward Sodom.
Two of the strangers went on ahead while the third, who was
actually the Lord, lingered awhile with Abraham. It was then
that Abraham received the crushing news. The Lord had come
with His two angels to destroy the wicked cities of Sodom and

Gomorrah. The sins of these two cities were so heinous and abundant that God could no longer tolerate their existence. They must be destroyed.

Immediately Abraham thought of Lot. He began to intercede with the Lord in Lot's behalf. After a typically oriental bargaining session, Abraham pled with the Lord not to destroy Sodom if ten righteous people could be found in it. The Lord agreed. However, there could not be found ten righteous citizens in this horribly wicked city and its destruction was certain. The angels prompted Lot to take his wife and two daughters and escape to the mountains. Lot fled, not to the mountains, but to the city of Zoar and as soon as he arrived the Lord rained fire and brimstone down upon Sodom and Gomorrah.

This fierce fire and brimstone that fell from Heaven not only destroyed the cities and their inhabitants but even the soil around them. The entire valley was burned out and utterly destroyed. It is likely that either the Dead Sea originated with this catastrophic event or that the existing sea was greatly enlarged to the south by engulfing this destroyed valley.

And what of Abraham? Is he resting comfortably in his tent while all this is going on? Not at all. Genesis 19:27 records, "And Abraham got up *early in the morning*" and viewed the smoke rising from the plain. He was genuinely interested in the welfare of Lot and his family and eagerly awaited news of them. The foolish nephew was spared from this devastation because God remembered the concern of Abraham.

Lot had slapped Abraham in the face by choosing the best land for himself. He had broken the heart of God's friend by settling in a center of wickedness. Abraham had every right to care nothing about Lot's welfare, yet he did care. He arose early, unselfishly, for he had learned not to seek his own but the good of others (1 Corinthians 10:24; Philippians 2:4). If you want to be happy today, why not spend the day helping others? Be interested in them; pray for them; bring good cheer to them. It will do a lot for you, too.

MORNING HYMN
> *Others, Lord, yes, others, Let this my motto be.*
> *Help me to live for others, That I might live like Thee.*

Waiting on God

MORNING SCRIPTURE Ruth 3-4
MORNING VERSE Ruth 3:13
Tarry this night, and it shall be in the morning, that if he will perform unto thee the part of a kinsman, well; let him do the kinsman's part: but if he will not do the part of a kinsman to thee, then will I do the part of a kinsman to thee, as the Lord liveth: lie down until the morning.

During our dark moments frequently we become impatient and ask God to speak to us immediately. But some times God is silent, and we must be silent as well. When the tears of frustration stream down our cheeks, when defeat and despair hang around us like a shroud, when we don't know which way to turn, we must heed God's advice to the psalmist, "Be still, and know that I am God" (Psalm 46:10).

Perhaps this divine stillness in the midst of the storm is best illustrated in the story of Ruth. A severe famine in Palestine drove Elimelech and Naomi, Ephrathites of Bethlehem, to Moab with their two sons, Mahlon and Chilion. Here the sons married Moabite girls named Ruth and Orpah. After ten years the father and sons died leaving three childless widows. Naomi decided to return to her homeland. Realizing the lonely life ahead for her daughters-in-law in a foreign country, she entreated them to remain behind in Moab. After some persuasion Orpah returned but Ruth requested, "Intreat me not to leave thee, or to return from following after thee: for whither thou goest, I will go; and where thou lodgest, I will lodge: thy people shall be my people and thy God my God" (Ruth 1:16). Hence, Ruth and Naomi traveled on together.

It was springtime during the barley harvest when Naomi and Ruth arrived in Bethlehem. Immediately Ruth went to glean in the field of a wealthy Ephrathite named Boaz, a relative of Elimelech, her father-in-law. Boaz showed kindness to Ruth, allowing her to eat with the Jews, contrary to the Hebrew custom, and eventually came to love her. Full of gratitude to God, Naomi instructed Ruth to claim her rights under the levirate law of marriage. This law, similar to those of the Assyrians and the Hittites, permitted a childless widow to marry her husband's brother or nearest kinsman in order to perpetuate the dead husband's name.

That night, when Boaz went to sleep, Ruth softly came and laid at his feet. During the night Boaz awoke and was startled to see Ruth. She identified herself and asked him to perform the duties of the near kinsman. Apparently Boaz's interest in Ruth had blossomed. However, he knew there was a kinsman nearer than he who must first be given the opportunity to perform this custom. Thus Boaz instructed Ruth, "Tarry this night, and it shall be *in the morning*, that if he will perform unto thee the part of the kinsman, well; let him do the kinsman's part; but if he will not do the part of the kinsman to thee, then will I do the part of the kinsman to thee, as the LORD liveth: lie down *until the morning*" (Ruth 3:13).

In the morning Ruth arose, was given six measures of barley by Boaz, and returned to the house of Naomi. Filled with anxiety over her future, Naomi instructed Ruth in the lesson of quiet faith. She said, "Sit still, my daughter, until thou know how the matter will fall." Boaz kept his word. He called ten witnesses of the elders to take their seats in the gate of the city to ratify his negotiations with the nearest kinsman to Ruth. When the kinsman refused to redeem his possession, that transferred the right of redemption legally to Boaz. Boaz and Ruth were married; she bore a son named Obed, the father of Jesse, the father of David. Good things happen to us when we sit still and wait on God.

Like Ruth, we must learn that no one who trusts God is ever forgotten by our Saviour. He is ever praying for us (Hebrews 7:25). We may feel forsaken and forlorn, but our High Priest is always touched with the feeling of our infirmities (Hebrews 4:15-16). He catches the tears of our anxiety and anguish alike "in [His] bottle" (Psalm 56:8). He is fully aware of our situation. In the meantime, we must simply sit still until we see how the matter will fall and learn the glorious lesson that, "They that wait upon the Lord shall renew their strength" (Isaiah 40:31).

MORNING HYMN

> *Be still, my soul: the Lord is on thy side;*
> *Bear patiently the cross of grief or pain*
> *Leave to thy God to order and provide*
> *In every change He faithful will remain.*

Satan's Imitators

MORNING SCRIPTURE   Exodus 7:1-25
MORNING VERSE   Exodus 7:15
Get thee unto Pharaoh in the morning; lo, he goeth out unto the water; and thou shalt stand by the river's brink against he come; and the rod which was turned to a serpent shalt thou take in thine hand.

Of all the brother teams in the Old Testament, Cain and Abel, Jacob and Esau, Hophni and Phinehas, etc., perhaps none was so outstanding as Moses and Aaron. Together they were called upon to undertake the impossible dream—the exodus of Israel from Egypt. Jehovah had made Moses a god to Pharaoh and brother Aaron was his prophet. As a team they stood before the Egyptian king and demanded the release of God's people Israel.

During the new kingdom period the power of Pharaoh was unsurpassed among contemporary nations. At times his kingdom extended as far as the Euphrates River. For Moses and Aaron to appear at the royal Egyptian court demanding that the people of Israel be set free was a challenge to Pharaoh's power. From the start the king's attitude was one of arrogant defiance. Pharaoh said, "Who is the LORD, that I should obey His voice to let Israel go? I know not the LORD, neither will I let Israel go" (Exodus 5:2).

But the Lord had forewarned Moses and Aaron of Pharaoh's attitude, informing them that when the king asked for a miracle to prove God's power they should cast Aaron's rod to the ground and it would become a serpent. When Pharaoh questioned them, Aaron obeyed God and, as God had promised, the rod miraculously became a serpent. However, much to the surprise of Moses and Aaron, the king of Egypt called upon his wise men and sorcerers to do the same and their rods too became serpents.

Apparently these Egyptian magicians knew the secret of paralyzing a snake by applying pressure on the back of the neck. This would make the serpent become rigid and the pompous

Egyptian sorcerers would stroll along the streets using the paralyzed snakes as walking sticks. When they cast the snake to the ground, releasing the pressure, the snake would begin to crawl. Capturing the snake was a simple matter of grabbing it by the back of the neck, renewing the pressure, and making the serpent rigid again.

Such was the case in the contest between Moses and Aaron and the magicians of Pharaoh's court. However, as the Egyptians imitated the miracle of God they did not have opportunity to grab the serpents by the back of the neck and reapply the pressure. Before they could do so Aaron's rod-serpent swallowed them up.

Rather than be stunned by the defeat of his magicians, Pharaoh's heart was hardened. Thus the Lord instructed Moses to "Get thee unto Pharaoh *in the morning*" and to demand that the people of Israel be released (Exodus 7:15). Early the next morning the confrontation took place and as a result of Pharaoh's refusal the Nile River, long worshiped by the Egyptians, turned to blood. Thus began the great plagues of Egypt.

Although in the first two plagues God allowed the Egyptian magicians to imitate His miracles, by the third one they had run out of tricks. Candidly they had to admit to Pharaoh, "This is the finger of God" (Exodus 8:19). This did not end imitations of God's power, however, for Satan is the great imitator of God. He has been imitating God through the centuries, and many have been deceived by some clever counterfeits which seem to be of God, but actually are of the devil.

Today the world is deluged with deception. Satan is on a rampage imitating the acts of God. This is why Christians are cautioned to "Believe not every spirit, but try the spirits whether they are of God; because many false prophets are gone out into the world" (1 John 4:1). Moses and Aaron were not fooled or intimidated by the imitation miracles of the Egyptian magicians. Believers today must not be fooled or intimidated by the power of Satan, "because greater is He that is in you, than he that is in the world" (1 John 4:4).

MORNING HYMN
> *Thy Holy Spirit, Lord, alone, Can turn our hearts from sin;*
> *His pow'r alone can sanctify, And keep us pure within.*

Wet Feet

MORNING SCRIPTURE   Joshua 3:1-17
MORNING VERSE   Joshua 3:1
And Joshua rose early in the morning; and they removed from Shittim, and came to Jordan, he and all the children of Israel, and lodged there before they passed over.

F aith is getting yourself in so deep that only God can get you out. This concept of faith is readily seen in the account of Joshua and the children of Israel as they crossed the Jordan River into the promised land.

With the passing of Moses a new servant of the Lord was commissioned to lead the chosen people of God. Joshua clearly had the promise of God that He would be with the Israelites. "Be strong and of good courage" (Joshua 1:6). "Only be thou strong and very courageous" (1:7). "Have not I commanded thee? Be strong and of good courage; be not afraid, neither be thou dismayed: for the LORD thy God is with thee whithersoever thou goest" (1:9). "Only be strong and of a good courage" (1:18). Armed with these promises of divine assistance, Joshua immediately sent two men into the land to spy out the city of Jericho. Here the spies met Rahab the harlot and their lives were spared by her hiding them from the king's men. After three days the spies returned to Joshua and reported that all the inhabitants of the land were afraid of the mighty Jehovah and that Israel could easily enter the land and establish a beachhead there.

As a decisive leader, Joshua wasted no time in mustering the Israelite camp. Joshua *rose early in the morning* (Joshua 3:1) and they removed from Shittim to the Jordan River. Roaring downward toward the Dead Sea, the mighty current of the Jordan is very strong at Jericho, especially during the harvest season. Because of the melting snows in the Lebanon mountains, and the overflowing of the Jordan during the month of Nisan (April), crossing the river at this season was regarded in ancient times as a very extraordinary feat. It is mentioned in 1 Chronicles 12:15 as a heroic act on the part of the brave Gaddites. Undoubtedly the rushing waters had overflowed the banks when the two spies crossed the river a few days before. But it was altogether impossible for the children of Israel with their wives and children to cross the mighty current. What was a great obstacle for man was a great opportunity for a miracle for the omnipotent God.

After Joshua rose early in the morning and commanded the people to move to the water's edge, they abode there three days. Here they were given instructions as to how to proceed across the water and told to sanctify themselves, "for tomorrow the LORD will do wonders among you" (Joshua 3:5). In the morning, as commanded, the priests of Israel led the procession to the brink of Jordan's waters. Miraculously when the priest entered the water, bearing the ark of the covenant, the mighty Jordan River "stood upon an heap."

Faith that had faltered at Kadesh forty years before was now tested again. When God caused the parting of the waters of the Red Sea, it was for Israel to escape with their lives from the pursuit of the Egyptian foe. Now, however, Israel was on the march and the foe was on the other side of the river. But the crossing of the Jordan was more of an act of faith than the crossing of the Red Sea. Upon leaving Egypt the Israelites saw God part the waters before they entered them. But now the waters were not parted. Not until the soles of the priests' feet touched the water was the river rolled back. It was not an act of obedience following what God had already done, but an act of faith which caused the priests to enter the swift current of the mighty Jordan.

We should never fear God's leading, even into the turbulent Jordans of our lives, for God stands behind His commands with His omnipotence. Trusting God is taking that step of faith. Trust Him today for today's step of faith.

MORNING HYMN

> *Encamped along the hills of light,*
> *Ye Christian soldiers, rise,*
> *And press the battle ere the night*
> *Shall veil the glowing skies.*
> *Against the foe in vales below*
> *Let all our strength be hurled;*
> *Faith is the victory, we know,*
> *That overcomes the world.*

Practical Religion

MORNING SCRIPTURE   Matthew 16:1-28
MORNING VERSE   Matthew 16:3
And in the morning, It will be foul weather to day: for the sky is red and lowring. O ye hypocrites, ye can discern the face of the sky; but can ye not discern the signs of the times?

F aith in Jesus Christ as Saviour transforms us from a shallow meaningless person into one filled with the Spirit of God. If we are born again and the Spirit resides within us, our religion ought to be as full of meaning as our lives are full of the Spirit. How terrible to see many religions in which there is absolute meaninglessness because of spiritual ritualism. Jesus encountered this very same thing in His day as well.

The Pharisees were always guilty of practicing an empty religion. This is why John the Baptist called them a "generation of vipers" (Matthew 3:7). The Pharisees were constantly interested in keeping the ceremonial law, but they had the wrong heart attitude toward God. When Jesus called Matthew to discipleship, the Pharisees were right there to question the Lord's disciples, "Why eateth your Master with publicans and sinners?" (Matthew 9:11). When He cast a demon out of a man who was dumb, the Pharisees accused Jesus of casting out devils through the power of the prince of the devils (Matthew 9:34).

Always the Pharisees were seeking a sign from Jesus that He was the Messiah. Time and again He refused to give them such a sign saying that the sign of Jonah was all they would need. His resurrection after a death of three days would be the great sign to them that He was indeed the Messiah. If they would not believe that sign, neither would they believe any other.

At Magdala Jesus again encountered the Pharisees, this time in league with the Sadducees and Herodians, who again asked Him for a sign. As before, Jesus refused to give them such a sign but at the same time He taught them something about the emptiness and blindness of their spiritual ritualism. Jesus noted that the Pharisees and Sadducees could read the weather signs in the heavens. He said, "When it is evening you say, it will be fair weather for the sky is red." This is comparable to our axiom,

"Red sky at night, sailor's delight." But Jesus continued, "And *in the morning* it will be foul weather to day: for the sky is red and lowring" (Matthew 16:3). Or, as we would say, "Red sky in morning, sailors take warning." Jesus then concluded with the assessment, "O ye hypocrites, ye can discern the face of the sky; but can ye not discern the signs of the times?" These religious leaders could read the skies with the best astronomers and mariners, but could not recognize that Jesus was the Messiah. This was where their expertise should have been, but because they had been involved so long with empty formalism instead of meaningful activity in carrying God's love to the world, they did not have the eyes of faith with which to see Jesus as their Saviour.

An item from a church bulletin clearly points out the inconsistency of pious religion which does not follow through in meeting the needs of people. It is a satirical rephrasing of Matthew 25: "I was famished and you formed a humanitarian club to discuss my hunger...I was imprisoned and you crept off quietly to your church to pray for my release. I was naked and you debated the morality of my unseemly appearance. I was sick and you knew it, yet did nothing but thank God for your own health. I was homeless and you preached to me of the spiritual shelter of the love of God. I was lonely and you left me by myself while you went and prayed for me. You seemed so holy, so close to God; but I am still very hungry, desolate, and cold!"

While the Pharisees had all the trappings of religion, all the robes, all the religious paraphernalia, they had none of the heart, none of what true religion is all about. Yet today as well there are many churches and denominations that have all the trappings of religion but none of the heart of the Lord Jesus. It is up to each of us to make sure that we attend faithfully those churches which show the heart of the Lord Jesus and not the heart of the Pharisee. Is your church following Jesus or following the Pharisees? Is your religion practical? Make it a point to pray for your church today.

MORNING HYMN
> *All Thy works with joy surround Thee,*
> *Earth and Heav'n reflect Thy rays,*
> *Stars and angels sing around Thee,*
> *Center of unbroken praise.*

A Lapse into Sin

MORNING SCRIPTURE   Genesis 20:1-18
MORNING VERSE   Genesis 20:8
Therefore Abimelech rose early in the morning, and called all his servants, and told all these things in their ears: and the men were sore afraid.

Our folly and God's grace; if you see one can the other be far behind? Frequent are the occasions when God's children foolishly mire themselves in difficulty only to have God graciously dig them out. Even the venerable Abraham found himself in this situation more than once.

After the destruction of Sodom and Gomorrah, Abraham departed from the groves of Mamre and journeyed south to the Negev. Here he dwelt between Kadesh and Shur, pitching his tent in Gerar. Upon arriving in the south country Abraham hatched a plan which he had tried unsuccessfully in Egypt some twenty years earlier. He instructed his wife, Sarah, to claim that she was his sister.

Because of the disastrous consequences which it previously had brought on the pharaoh of Egypt, it is almost inconceivable that Abraham would try this scheme again. Apparently the stern rebuke Abraham received from pharaoh had by this time faded from his memory. Still, Abraham had only recently received God's assurance that Sarah was destined to be the mother of the promised seed. By spreading the half truth that she was his sister and therefore eligible for marriage, Abraham placed Sarah's virtue in serious jeopardy. This constituted a foolish lapse in Abraham's usually stellar performance as the friend of God.

The arrival of Abraham and Sarah brought a greeting from Abimelech, the warlike king of Gerar. Having heard that Sarah was unmarried, Abimelech immediately sent and brought her into his harem. This likely was done to ally himself with the rich nomad prince, Abraham. Sarah was by this time ninety years old and probably not the beautiful maid she used to be. Suddenly Abraham's lie had come back to haunt him once again.

The whole course of human history could have been different if it were not for God's intervention. Genesis 20:3 begins, "But God," words which usually indicate the turning point between man's foolishness and God's grace. Abraham had lied about his wife and she was now part of Abimelech's harem. Her virtue would undoubtedly be violated. But God warned the Philistine king in a dream that Sarah was already a man's wife. He also caused Abimelech to be afflicted with an illness which prevented him from coming near Sarah. Thus, miraculously and graciously, the mother of the chosen nation was kept from impurity, not because of the wisdom of Abraham, but because of the grace of God.

In the dream God revealed to Abimelech that, although he had done no wrong, nevertheless he must restore Sarah to her husband. If the king refused, his death and that of all his kingdom would ensue. This was enough to convince Abimelech. The king *"rose early in the morning,* and called all his servants," relaying the message to them (Genesis 20:8). Respecting the authority of the living God, Abimelech was anxious to heed the divine directives. The Philistine wasted no time in returning Sarah to her husband but not without a sharp rebuke to Abraham. Happy to have his wife back safe and sound, Abraham received the reprimand with a sigh of relief. In return he prayed to God and Abimelech was healed along with his wife and maidservants. The kingdom returned to normal.

Once again God's grace had prevailed over man's folly. The results could have been drastically different, however, had not God's providence overruled man's foolishness. Yet, how much anguish could have been spared both Abraham and Abimelech, both Sarah and the Philistine's wife, if there had not been that one lapse from righteousness. The knowledge that God's grace is waiting in the wings is insufficient grounds for contemplating foolish action. As Abraham finally learned, every friend of God must carefully guard against even slight lapses into the folly of sin (Romans 6:1-4).

MORNING HYMN
> *Sinners Jesus will receive;*
> *Sound this word of grace to all*
> *Who the heav'nly pathway leave,*
> *All who linger, all who fall.*

Skylight

MORNING SCRIPTURE   Psalm 5:1-12
MORNING VERSE   Psalm 5:3
*My voice shalt Thou hear in the morning, O LORD; in the morning
will I direct my prayer unto Thee, and will look up.*

A lthough the psalms sometimes depict men in the depths
of despair, they also frequently depict those same men
after they have risen to the heights of praise. It is this
tension between the depths and heights which gives vitality to
the psalms. When man views his own circumstances, he is given
to despair; when he views God's deliverance, he is given to
praise. The difference is his vision of God.

When Noah was commanded to build his strange-looking
craft, he was instructed by God to make only one window in
the entire ship. The window was to be in the roof (Genesis 6:16).
There was just one way for Noah to look out of his craft, and
that was up. The opening in the ark was actually a skylight toward Heaven.

Here in Psalm 5 David has learned the same lesson that
God taught Noah. He exclaims, "My voice shalt Thou hear in
the morning, O LORD; in the morning will I direct my prayer
unto Thee, and will look up" (Psalm 5:3).

There are two things worthy of our attention in this verse.
First, the posture of David in prayer being that *in the morning*
"will I direct my prayer unto thee." The verb chosen by the
psalmist is a military term and means that morning after morning he would marshal his prayers, he would set them in battle
array. His prayer life was not a haphazard one, but one characterized by consistency and seriousness of purpose. To the psalmist, praying to God was as serious as planning a campaign
against the enemy.

Second, notice the practice of the psalmist after his prayer.
Once he had completed marshaling his prayer to God, he promised that he would "look up." Again a military term is used.
Once David had set his prayers in rank and file, in good military order, he then resolved to look abroad, to look toward the
door of God in anticipation of the answer to his prayers.

Here is the great lesson of faith. It does us no good to pray to God if we do not anticipate that God will answer our prayers. If you do not believe, why do you pray? And if you do believe, why do you not expect God to answer you? When you pray you are showing your dependence upon God. When you do not expect God to answer you, you are renouncing your confidence in Him. It was the Puritan writer Thomas Brooks who said, "He is either a fool or a madman, he is either very weak or very wicked that prays and prays, but never looks after his prayers; that shoots many an arrow toward Heaven, but never minds where his arrows alight."

The secret of a faithful prayer life is not to spend our time foolishly fretting about the storms which surround our ship, but, having taken note of those storms, to commit our ship to the great Captain of the seas. It is not the severity of the storm that is important, but the capability of the Captain. The lesson we must learn is to keep looking up to Jesus instead of looking around at our trials.

As believers we are in the "ark of salvation," though we are yet adrift in a stormy world of sin and sorrow. We are commanded to look up rather than to allow our hearts to be overwhelmed by the circumstances around us. Faith fills the soul with expectation. Hence, we not only direct our prayers to God but we look up toward Him in anticipation of an answer. Prayerful expectation allows us to cash in on the credits of God's promise.

When you live with a "skylight" perspective you will find answered prayer becoming a delightful habit in your life. Don't allow the day to go by without directing your prayer to God and looking to Him in anticipation of His answer. Do it in the morning and you will have a day filled with expectation.

MORNING HYMN

> *My faith looks up to Thee,*
> *Thou Lamb of Calvary,*
> *Saviour divine!*
> *Now hear me while I pray,*
> *Take all my guilt away,*
> *O let me from this day*
> *Be wholly Thine!*

God's "Haves" and "Wills"

MORNING SCRIPTURE   Joshua 5:13-6:16
MORNING VERSE   Joshua 6:12
And Joshua rose early in the morning, and the priests took up the ark of the LORD.

As they had miraculously left the land of Egypt, Israel had now entered the land of Canaan by a similar miracle. All the people were safely across the swift waters of the Jordan. The army of Israel encamped at Gilgal. Having settled in the land, Joshua and the people were now ready for their first great test—the capture of the outpost of Jericho.

Since Jericho was the most secure stronghold in a string of fortifications defending the eastern front of Canaan, there were many anxious Israelite hearts the night before the conquest began. Joshua himself was pacing the ground at the edge of the Israeli encampment. While meditating on how to attack Jericho, a man appeared to Joshua with a sword drawn in his hand. Intrepidly Joshua asked, "Art thou for us, or for our adversaries?" (Joshua 5:14) The powerful figure identified himself as the Captain of the host of the Lord. This title, so often afterward applied to the Son of God, revealed to Joshua that this was none other than the Lord Jesus Christ. Joshua must have known immediately the identity of this warrior for he fell on his face to the earth and worshiped Him.

Joshua 6:2 records, "And the LORD said unto Joshua, See, I have given into thine hand Jericho, and the king thereof, and the mighty men of valor." Although it was the night before the once-a-day treks around the city of Jericho, the Lord's promise to Joshua was, "I have given into thine hand Jericho, and the king thereof." Their lines of battle had not yet been drawn. The fighting had not yet begun. Yet the victory was certain. Even before the event occurred, God said "I have done it."

How can this be? How can God say the battle is won before it is begun? The answer is that God is above time. He has no futures nor pasts, only an eternal present. He always deals in what is for Him the "now." Frequently God uses the words "I will" and "I have" interchangeably.

Consider the similar experience of Abraham, recorded in Genesis 17. Abram was ninety-nine years old when the Lord God appeared to him and, as Joshua did, he fell on his face before the Lord. The Almighty God was about to make a covenant with Abram that he would become the father of many nations. To Abraham God said, "Neither shall thy name anymore be called Abram, but thy name shall be Abraham; for a father of many nations have I made thee" (Genesis 17:5). To a childless ninety-nine-year-old man, whose wife was nearly that age, God said, "A father of many nations have I made thee."

In quoting that promise in Romans 4:17, the Apostle Paul notes, "And being not weak in faith, he considered not his own body now dead, when he was about an hundred years old, neither yet the deadness of Sarah's womb" (Romans 4:19). It did not matter that Sarah was well beyond the age of childbearing. God said He had made Abraham the father of many nations and we can count God's "wills" as God's "haves."

As twentieth century believers, the promises of God to us which have yet to be fulfilled are in the eternality of God already fulfilled. Thus the Lord Jesus promised, "I go to prepare a place for you. And if I go and prepare a place for you, I will come again (John 14:2-3)." Although this is an event in history future, nevertheless, it is a promise as certain as if it had already been fulfilled. God calls things that are not yet as if they already are.

Hence, even though the battle plan was strange to Joshua, the defeat of the enemy was sure. Trusting the God of completed promises, "Joshua rose early in the morning, and the priests took up the ark of the LORD" (Joshua 6:12) and the children of Israel proceeded to the conquest of Jericho. Another great victory was won for the Lord God whose "haves" and "wills" are interchangeable.

MORNING HYMN
> *Be still, my soul: thy God doth undertake*
> *To guide the future as He has the past.*
> *Thy hope, thy confidence let nothing shake;*
> *All now mysterious shall be bright at last.*

Divine Direction

MORNING SCRIPTURE   Numbers 9:2-23
MORNING VERSE   Numbers 9:21
And so it was, when the cloud abode from even unto the morning, and that the cloud was taken up in the morning, then they journeyed: whether it was by day or by night that the cloud was taken up, they journeyed.

Each of us who is active and aggressive in our service for the Lord finds one aspect of the Christian life more difficult than any other. We find it almost impossible just to sit still and not to move when God is not moving us. The best antidote for anxiety is to trust in God and wait patiently on Him.

The movement of the nation of Israel through the wilderness graphically illustrates the need for God's people to wait on Him. Numbers 9 gives God's program for Israel's progression. The Jews were not on a steady march for forty years in the wilderness, neither were they at permanent rest. In fact, their journey was a long series of stops and gos. Both were at the command of God.

God never leaves His people alone, without a witness or guide. Living by faith sometimes means walking in the dark, but it never means living without a light. God would provide the natural phenomena of a cloud and fire. On the day that it was erected, a cloud covered the Tabernacle so that it was entirely enshrouded during the day. At night fire appeared in the sky and prohibited Israel from losing sight of the abode of God. Numbers 9:21 summarizes, "And so it was, when the cloud abode from even *unto the morning,* and that the cloud was taken up *in the morning* then they journeyed: whether it was by day or by night that the cloud was taken up, they journeyed." Since the length of the stay at any one place in the wilderness could vary from two days, to a month, to a year, Israel's only obligation was to trust God and watch for the movement of the cloud.

Many are the occasions that we find ourselves awaiting direction from the Lord and wondering if it will ever come. But if we let Him be our guide, we will not only "Rest in the LORD and wait patiently for Him" (Psalm 37:7), but when He does move us we will be certain that our direction is the correct one.

Some years ago a party of fisherman took their small boat into the Gulf of Mexico. They came to their favorite spot, a place they had been many times before. The weather was balmy, the fish were biting, and they completely lost themselves in the hours of the afternoon. By nightfall a dense fog had moved in and they found themselves completely engulfed in the "soup" and could see only a few feet ahead of them. Their hearts raced with excitement. Then one of the fishermen remembered that he had a small compass in his pocket. They had already determined which direction they should go, but the compass pointed in the opposite direction. Now they were faced with a dilemma. Would they follow their own instincts, or the sure rule of the compass? All the men agreed to follow the direction of the compass. After what seemed an endlessly long time, they saw the shadowy outline of the shore emerging through the fog. They found themselves only a few yards from the dock where they started earlier in the day. The reliable compass had told them which direction to go, they trusted it, and they returned home safely.

Let us not be guilty today of attempting to move ahead of God when He says to "sit still." Likewise, when through the Word of God we are moved in a particular direction, let us not question that direction, but do the will of God. The clouds of concern may completely encircle us today but God will remove them in His own good time and will provide direction for us if we simply trust Him and wait upon Him.

MORNING HYMN
> *Lord, I would clasp Thy hand in mine,*
> *Nor ever murmur nor repine,*
> *Content, whatever lot I see,*
> *Since 'tis my God that leadeth me!*

Morning Corruption

MORNING SCRIPTURE Zephaniah 1:1-3:20
MORNING VERSE Zephaniah 3:7
I said, Surely thou wilt fear me, thou wilt receive instruction; so their dwelling should not be cut off, howsoever I punished them: but they rose early, and corrupted all their doings.

Zephaniah is a book of contrasts. Perhaps no other prophecy in the Old Testament paints a blacker picture of God's judgment than does Zephaniah. It is a foreboding portrait of the day of Jehovah, the day of the Lord. Still, no prophet paints a brighter picture of Israel's future glory.

Zephaniah was a unique prophet. A contemporary of Jeremiah, more is known about the pedigree of Zephaniah than any other prophet. This first verse of this prophecy shows that his lineage was in the royal line; he was the great-great-grandson of good King Hezekiah. His royal heritage makes Zephaniah's rebuke of the nobles and princes all the more significant. He spoke to Judah and Jerusalem as one of their own, as royalty.

Taking occasion from the threat of invasion by the savage Scythian hordes from the north, Zephaniah preached of the coming of the great day of judgment on Judah and Jerusalem. With all the fervor of a revivalist, Zephaniah announced, "The great day of the LORD is near…. That day is a day of wrath, a day of trouble and distress, a day of wasteness and desolation, a day of darkness and gloominess, a day of clouds and thick darkness…. And I will bring distress upon men, that they shall walk like blind men, because they have sinned against the LORD; and their blood shall be poured out as dust…. Neither their silver nor their gold shall be able to deliver them in the day of the LORD's wrath…for He shall make even a speedy riddance of all them that dwell in the land" (Zephaniah 1:14-18).

In the three chapters of this tiny book nearly every word is laced with a warning about God's wrath. In chapter 1 the utter desolation of Judah is predicted as a judgment for idolatry and neglect of the Lord. In chapter 2 Zephaniah predicts that the house of Judah as well as her enemies, Moab and Ammon, will be threatened with perpetual destruction. In chapter 3 he turns his attention to the city of Jerusalem, calling it "filthy and polluted" and "the oppressing city."

Hurling invectives at Jerusalem's princes, her judges, her prophets, and her priests, Zephaniah warns that "the just LORD is in the midst thereof; He will not do iniquity: *every morning* doth He bring His judgment to light, He faileth not" (Zephaniah 3:5). Literally, morning by morning God will bring His judgment on the wicked city of Jerusalem. No one who defies the Lord God ever escapes punishment. Still, the princes, prophets, priests, and inhabitants of Jerusalem paid no attention to Zephaniah's warning. Instead, *"they rose early* and corrupted all their doings" (Zephaniah 3:7).

Although this section of Zephaniah's prophecy ends with the failure of the people to heed his warnings, nonetheless the prophet concludes with a series of promises (Zephaniah 3:8-20). The general tone of this last portion is messianic, speaking of the day when Christ will gather the nations and assemble His kingdoms, the day in which He will be in the midst of Jerusalem on Mount Zion, and the faithful remnant of Israel will rejoice and sing praises unto Him.

Zephaniah's life as a prophet was a miserable one; he was unheeded and mocked. Still, the future fulfillment of all his prophecies will grant him eternal vindication. It would be Zephaniah's prayer that none of us today rise early to corrupt our ways. Let's answer his prayer.

MORNING HYMN

For the Lord our God shall come
And shall take His harvest home:
From His field shall in that day
All offenses purge away—
Give His angels charge at last
In the fire the tares to cast
But the fruitful ears to store
In His garner evermore.

God's Separation

MORNING SCRIPTURE   Exodus 8:1-32
MORNING VERSE   Exodus 8:20
And the LORD said unto Moses, Rise up early in the morning, and stand before Pharaoh; lo, he cometh forth to the water; and say unto him, Thus saith the LORD, Let My people go, that they may serve Me.

I n a great many respects the righteous and unrighteous appear to be treated alike in this life. God "maketh His sun to rise on the evil and on the good, and sendeth rain on the just and on the unjust" (Matthew 5:45). However, lest the righteous begin feeling sorry for themselves, we must not forget that a day of separation is coming when the Shepherd will divide His sheep from the goats (Matthew 25:31-33). The sun will not forever rise on the unrighteous.

But if we look more closely, even in this life God puts a division between His people and those of the world. Satan complained that God had made a hedge around Job. Solomon said that the Lord "is a shield to those who walk uprightly. He keepeth the paths of justice, and preserveth the way of His saints" (Proverbs 2:7-8).

A prime example of the Lord's protection for His people is the plagues of Egypt. After his death, there arose a king over Egypt who knew not Joseph. The Israelites became slaves with taskmasters set over them to afflict them. Moses was called of God to lead the Jews out of this land of bondage and into the promised land. But when Moses and Aaron confronted the Egyptian king about letting God's people go, the pharaoh only increased the burden on the Jews. The ruler hardened his heart and there began in Egypt a series of plagues the likes of which have not been seen since anywhere in the world.

First, their water supply turned to blood. Then frogs covered the land. Next, it was the plague of lice or gnats. After this the Lord said to Moses, *"Rise up early in the morning,* and stand before Pharaoh" (Exodus 8:20). The man of God warned the Egyptian king that if he would not let God's people go, the land would become black with flies.

These were not ordinary houseflies but horseflies. They are described by the historian Philo and other travelers as a very severe scourge. More numerous and annoying than houseflies, these gadflies fasten themselves to the human body, especially around the edges of the eyelids, and suck blood from the agonized victim. They would swarm and fill the houses of the Egyptians causing severe pain and distress.

But here for the first time an additional promise is made. God said He would set apart the land of Goshen, where His people Israel dwelt, and absolutely no swarm of flies would enter there. A division between God's people and the people of Egypt was to be formed. In fact, this division meant redemption. God would redeem Israel and protect them from the devastating swarm.

The Bible clearly indicates the purpose of this division was "to the end thou mayest know that I am the Lord in the midst of the earth." God's setting apart of the land of Goshen was calculated to impress the worldly Egyptians that Jehovah alone is God. This was no trick of Egyptian magic; it was the direct intervention of God in human affairs. Jehovah caused a plague to fall on the unrighteous and peace to fall on the righteous.

Even today the Lord is separating a people for His name. The believer is set apart as a testimony to the world that Jehovah is God and He is in absolute control of the universe. God's people are to be a distinct and blessed group, in the world but not of it. We are set apart from the penalty of sin that plagues the world around us. Likewise we are set apart unto service for the God who saved us. Let's praise Him today for His grace in our behalf.

MORNING HYMN
> *O God, our help in ages past,*
> *Our hope for years to come,*
> *Our shelter from the stormy blast,*
> *And our eternal home!*

Persistence

MORNING SCRIPTURE   Daniel 6:1-28
MORNING VERSE   Daniel 6:19
Then the king arose very early in the morning, and went in haste unto the den of lions.

We have all heard the adage, "Persistence pays." There is one striking example in Scripture, however, when persistence did more than pay. In the case of Daniel, persistence prospered.

The golden years of the Persian Empire were those of Darius the Great. Darius extended the empire from India to the Danube River, even to Greece itself. He also commanded his governors to aid in the rebuilding of the Temple at Jerusalem (Ezra 6:1-12). In his desire to rule well his kingdom, Darius set one hundred twenty princes over the whole kingdom as viceregents. Over these were three presidents, of whom Daniel was the first. Daniel's prosperity as first president evoked the jealousy of the other presidents, who sought to destroy him. So godly was this man that the only way he could be destroyed was through wretched trickery.

The presidents knew that Daniel would not forsake the law of his God and therefore they proposed an unalterable decree that no one should pray to any person other than the king for a period of thirty days. Unaware of their vicious intent, King Darius signed the decree.

Although Daniel knew that the law had been signed, nonetheless he continued his practice of kneeling before a window opened toward Jerusalem and giving thanks to the Lord three times a day. His envious colleagues laid in wait to catch Daniel forsaking the unalterable law of the Medes and Persians. When they advised the king that Daniel had disregarded his decree, the king was greatly distressed, for he thought highly of Daniel. Nevertheless, he followed through on the punishment for disobeying his decree and cast Daniel into the den of lions. A stone was brought and laid over the mouth of the den so Daniel could not escape. His death was inevitable.

Throughout the night the king could not sleep, nor could his mind be soothed with music. He arose *very early in the morning* and went quickly to the den of lions (Daniel 6:19). Much to his amazement, Jehovah God had spared the life of Daniel and shut the lions' mouths. The king was glad to receive Daniel out of the lions' den safe and sound. After punishing those who had falsely accused Daniel, Darius wrote a decree to all nations that the God of Daniel should be revered and respected as the living God.

The persistent prayer of Daniel may be viewed as a foolish practice, given the law of the Medes and the Persians. But persistence in godliness is never persistence in foolishness. In fact, persistence in doing what is right always leads to prosperity.

A South Carolina man passing out tracts once stopped at a house and rang the bell. He heard noises inside and knew that someone was in there, but no one came to the door. He rang the bell persistently. Finally a man appeared, grabbed the tract from his hand, and rudely slammed the door in his face.

A week later the Christian returned to that door and this time the man received him immediately. After he entered the house, the man took him to the attic to see a rope dangling from the rafters with a box beneath it. The man of the house said, "Friend, when you rang my doorbell last week, my head was in that noose, and I was ready to jump! But you were so persistent that I decided to go down and see who it was. While reading your tract God spoke to me. Instead of jumping off that box, I knelt beside it and gave my heart to the Lord."

Like Daniel of old, who was persistent in doing what is right, this Christian's persistence in ringing that doorbell led to another man's salvation. Regardless of what men may think, persistence in doing what is right always brings the prosperity of God.

MORNING HYMN
> *Truehearted, wholehearted, faithful and loyal,*
> *King of our lives, by Thy grace we will be;*
> *Under the standard exalted and royal,*
> *Strong in Thy strength we will battle for Thee.*

Discouragement

MORNING SCRIPTURE   Judges 6:1-32
MORNING VERSE   Judges 6:28
*And when the men of the city arose early in the morning, behold,
the altar of Baal was cast down, and the grove was cut down that
was by it, and the second bullock was offered upon the altar that
was built.*

T he book of Judges recounts the history of Israel during
the centuries which followed the conquest of the land of
Canaan. These were checkered years in Israel's history,
which frequently saw relapses into idolatry. After each time Israel turned aside from the Lord, Jehovah would graciously raise
up a judge, who was a military not a judicial leader, to bring His
chosen people back to Him. The cycle of relapse, repentance, and
restoration occurred frequently during these turbulent centuries.

The narrative of Judges 6 opens with a record of the renewed
idolatry of Israel. This time judgment came from the Midianites
who swept down through the plain of Jezreel, terrorizing Israel
as far south as Gaza. They did not permanently occupy the land,
but each harvest season would arrive unexpectedly and plunder
the harvest. What spoil they could not carry away they destroyed.
So insecure were the Israelites that they lived in dens, caves, and
strongholds to seek safety for their possessions and for themselves.

But suddenly things changed. An angel of the Lord appeared
under the great oak by Ophrah, a little township on the southwest-
ern border of the territory of Manasseh. There Gideon, the son of
Joash, was beating out wheat with a stick. He did so secretly and
with constant apprehension that a wild band of Midianite bedouin
might sweep down on him, taking his grain and his life.

Gideon is typical of many believers today. Although the angel of the Lord called him a "mighty man of valor," Gideon's clan-
destine operations at his father's winepress did not exhibit great
valor. For seven years his people had been oppressed by the enemy and this mighty warrior was despondent and discouraged.
The angel of the Lord appeared unto him at his lowest ebb to
encourage him.

Gideon was startled at first by this stranger, not certain who he was. When the angel proclaimed that the Lord was with him, Gideon's questioning response was, "If the LORD be with us, why then is all this befallen us?" (Judges 6:13) Gideon believed that if Jehovah had not withdrawn Himself from Israel, the present Midianite calamity would never have occurred. As well, this mighty man of valor, like Moses of old, questioned why the Lord would choose him to deliver Israel. His family was poor in Manasseh and he was the least of his father's household. But in the midst of Gideon's concern the Lord God promised, "Surely I will be with thee, and thou shalt smite the Midianites as one man."

Gideon was still not convinced. How did he know this person was really the angel of the Lord? Thus Gideon asked for a sign and the angel of the Lord flash-fired the flesh of a kid and unleavened cakes which Gideon had placed on a rock.

Having felt the hand of God upon his life and claiming the promise of divine presence and power, Gideon proceeded to be the delivering judge of Israel. At the command of the Lord he threw down the altar of Baal his father had built. In its place he built an altar unto Jehovah God. "And when the men of the city *arose early in the morning* behold, the altar of Baal was cast down, and the grove was cut down" (Judges 6:28). Who had done such a thing? The answer—Gideon, the son of Joash. The fearful men of the city stormed the house of Joash and demanded that he hand over his son to be slain. But the acts of an encouraged Gideon bred encouragement in the heart of his father as well. Joash challenged the men to allow Baal to plead for himself, if he truly was a god. It was becoming increasingly evident to the men of Ophrah that Baal was not a god to be feared, as was Jehovah.

All that was necessary for a discouraged people to rise up against their oppressors was for the heart of one man to be impressed with the presence and power of the Lord. How much the Gideons of the twentieth century need to recognize the still small voice of the Lord saying to them, "Surely I will be with thee." Be encouraged and let God do something courageous through you today.

MORNING HYMN
Take my life and let it be, Consecrated, Lord, to Thee
Take my hands and let them move, At the impulse of Thy love,
Take my feet and let them be, Swift and beautiful for Thee;
Take my voice and let me sing, Always, only, for my King.

Mother's Prayers

MORNING SCRIPTURE   1 Samuel 1:1-2:11
MORNING VERSE   1 Samuel 1:19
And they rose up in the morning early, and worshiped before the LORD, and returned, and came to their house to Ramah: and Elkanah knew Hannah his wife; and the LORD remembered her.

N o greater blessing exists in life than to have a godly mother and nothing in this world is quite so heartening as to know that your mother is praying for you. Behind Moses was Jochebed; behind John the Baptist was Elizabeth; and behind Timothy was Eunice. But no account of a praying mother is quite so touching as that of Hannah.

The first book of Samuel begins with the story of an Ephraimite named Elkanah. Elkanah had two wives, an instance of polygamy which, like all the others in the Old Testament, engendered bitterness and jealously. One of Elkanah's wives, Peninnah, had borne him several children. The other wife, Hannah, was barren for "the LORD had shut up her womb" (1 Samuel 1:5).

During this period of Israel's history it was a rare sight to see such piety as was displayed by Elkanah and his wives. Yearly this man went with his family to Shiloh where the ark of the covenant was and where Eli ministered as high priest. There Elkanah sacrificed unto the Lord. Although Elkanah fairly treated both of his wives, and although Peninnah had given him offspring, he was especially attracted to Hannah and when it came time to offer his sacrifice unto the Lord he gave her a double portion of the offering. There is nothing in the text that would indicate Hannah in any way flaunted before Peninnah this double portion or the affection of Elkanah. Nonetheless Peninnah, described as her "adversary," sorely provoked Hannah year after year and taunted her because she was childless. Such jealous provocation by her rival caused Hannah to lose her appetite and weep sorely.

So great was the bitterness of her soul because she was barren that Hannah earnestly sought the Lord and His blessing on her life. She vowed a vow that if the Lord would give her a son she would give him back to the Lord in service. Her true piety is seen in her ability to shut out the rest of the world as she prayed to God. Hannah opened her heart to God, but not her lips. She spoke privately and fervently to the only one who could give her the desire of her heart. In faith believing, she committed her barrenness to God and with a sorrowful spirit sought release from that barrenness. When Eli the high priest learned of her request he sent her away in peace with the prayer, "The God of Israel grant thee thy petition that thou hast asked of Him." Having taken her burden to the Lord, Hannah left it there.

They rose up in the morning early, Elkanah and his two wives, worshiped before the Lord, and returned to their home in Ramah (1 Samuel 1:19). Soon Hannah's prayers were answered. She conceived and bore a son, Samuel, whom she returned to Shiloh and to the service of the Lord as promised. Hannah's prayers began before her son's life began but they did not cease when she gave him back to the Lord. She continued to pray with unfailing regularity for God's blessing on His gift to her and her gift to Him.

"Twas in the days of long ago when life was fair and bright, and scarce a fear and ne'er a tear o'ercast my day and night, but often in the eventide I found her kneeling there, and just one word—my name I heard—my name in mother's prayer. I wandered on and heeded not God's oft-repeated call to turn from sin—to live for Him—to give to Him my all; until at last of sin convinced I sank in deep despair, and hope awoke and memory spoke my name in mother's prayer. That pleading heart, that soul so tried, has gone into her rest, but still with me for aye shall be the memory of her trust. And when I reach the Golden Shore and meet her over there, we'll praise the Lord who blessed that word—my name in mother's prayer!"

Two things must never be underestimated in this life. The first is the love of God; the second is the influence of a mother's prayer. Mothers, pray for your children this morning. Pray for them by name and by need. Only eternity will reveal the results.

MORNING HYMN

I'm coming home, I'm coming home,
To live my wasted life anew,
For mother's prayers have followed me,
Have followed me the whole world through.

Practical Wisdom

MORNING SCRIPTURE   1 Kings 3:1-28
MORNING VERSE   1 Kings 3:21
And when I rose in the morning to give my child suck, behold, it was dead: but when I had considered it in the morning, behold, it was not my son, which I did bear.

How much better is it to get wisdom than gold! And to get understanding rather to be chosen than silver" (Proverbs 16:16). These sentiments of Solomon, regarding the preference for wisdom over wealth, stem from a strange dream that changed his life.

Once Solomon attended a solemn procession to the altar at Gibeon, about five miles from Jerusalem. This is where the ancient Tabernacle yet stood. Here the king celebrated an elaborate religious festival in which he offered a thousand burnt offerings on the altar built by Bezaleel nearly five centuries before. While at Gibeon, Solomon received a dream from the Lord, in which God demanded, "Ask what I shall give thee" (1 Kings 3:5). Solomon barely knew what to request from God. Then he remembered the great task that had been laid before him. He was the king of the chosen nation, a great people that could not be numbered for their multitude. Solomon asked for practical wisdom, the ability to discern between right and wrong and to make immediate judgments that were founded on the truth. He was not asking for spiritual discernment; he wanted to rule the people well. God was pleased with Solomon's concern to be a just ruler and thus granted Solomon's request and added riches, honor, and length of days as well.

An occasion soon arose to test this divine gift of practical wisdom. Two harlots came before the king bearing two children, one dead, one alive. Although their stories were conflicting, they did agree both lived in the same house and recently, within days of one another, each gave birth to a child. One woman claimed that the dead child was the result of the other mother's carelessness in accidentally laying on the child during the night and suffocating it. She claimed that the other woman rose at midnight, took her living son from beside her, and placed the dead infant in its stead. When the woman arose *in the morning* to feed the child, she discovered it was dead (1 Kings 3:21). She also discovered in the morning, at the light of day, that it was not her child lifelessly lying beside her in bed. She claimed that the living child was hers. The other woman disputed the claim saying that the first woman's child had simply died and she was now trying to compensate for her loss by taking the live child to be her own.

The situation appeared hopeless. It was the perfect test for Solomon's practical wisdom. What would he do? The king resolved to appeal to the maternal instinct of the women. He called for a sword to "divide the living child in two, and give half to the one, and half to the other." Immediately the child's mother screamed and requested that the king give her own child to the other woman rather than see him slain. Solomon thus discerned which woman was telling the truth and presented the child to his mother.

The fame of this decision spread throughout all Israel, inspiring fear of the king's justice and a conviction that God had given Solomon exceptional discernment. Israel believed that he would carry out his administrative duties with supreme justice.

Solomon's wisdom, however, appears to have gone beyond mere practical shrewdness in everyday affairs: 1 Kings 4:29-34 indicates Solomon demonstrated significant literary ability in speaking three thousand proverbs and writing more than one thousand psalms. One of those proverbs was, "Death and life are in the power of the tongue" (Proverbs 18:21). On this occasion, a happy mother had just realized the truth of those words.

MORNING HYMN
> *Hover o'er me, Holy Spirit,*
> *Bathe my trembling heart and brow;*
> *Fill me with thy hallow'd presence,*
> *Come, O come and fill me now.*

First Appointment

MORNING SCRIPTURE   Psalm 63:1-11
MORNING VERSE   Psalm 63:1
O God, Thou art my God; early will I seek Thee: my soul thirsteth for Thee, my flesh longeth for Thee in a dry and thirsty land, where no water is.

How amazing it is that finite creatures such as you and I may have fellowship with the infinite God. Yet this is our privilege as Christians; it is our right. But rights always bring responsibilities.

Psalm 63 is a gem of a morning psalm. The eloquent preacher of the fourth century, Chrysostom, testifies, "It was decreed and ordained by the primitive fathers, that no day should pass without the public singing of this psalm." It is easy to see why the early Christians sang this song aloud at the beginning of every day. They would start their song, "O God, Thou art my God." This is easy to say, but difficult to live. To say that God is our God conveys a great deal of benefit. Because He is our God, all that He has is ours as well. We are heirs of God and joint heirs with Jesus Christ (Romans 8:17). Ours is not an empty relationship with God but one filled with great blessing, great benefit, great privilege.

But all of us who claim the Lord as our God don't just receive special favors from Him; we return special services to Him. This is why in Psalm 118:28 David says, "Thou art my God, and I will praise Thee: Thou art my God, I will exalt Thee." Because He is our God and because we have special rights it is incumbent upon us to exercise certain responsibilities. This David recognizes when he says, "O God, Thou art my God: *early will I seek thee*" (Psalm 63:1).

While as servants of God we may claim interest in Him, we also must exhibit our duty toward Him. Before all things, at the dawn of every day, before we seek anyone else, before we have our breakfast, "early will I seek Thee."

There seems to be a direct relationship between seeking God in the morning and success throughout the day. Dr. Andrew

Bonar once wrote in his diary: "Tonight I gave myself to a time of waiting upon the Lord. I had not been much in the spirit of prayer, but now several things have become clear to me. I realize I have not communed enough with the Lord, nor come to Him as often as I should. Little forethought has been given to the requests I've made. There has been much conversing and outward engagement with men, but I have not been occupied enough with God Himself. I also realize that a closeness to Him gives abundant strength and is like sunlight shining through the clouds on a gloomy day." Bonar recognized that had he sought the Lord early, at the beginning of his day, and walked with Him consistently throughout the day, his evening time of waiting on the Lord in prayer would have been much more productive. The same is true for each of us.

Satisfaction for the soul cannot be found apart from fellowship with the Lord. David the psalmist sought to maintain his companionship with God from early morning until late at night. He made a practice of being in the "presence" of God throughout the day by the blessed privilege of prayer.

When our souls thirst for the Lord as our parched tongues thirst for water, when our appetite for righteousness equals our appetite for food, then we will make it a habit of rising early in the morning to make our first appointment of the day an appointment with God. He will be the first one on our minds in the morning and the last one on our minds at night.

MORNING HYMN
> *When morning gilds the skies,*
> *My heart awaking cries;*
> *May Jesus Christ be praised;*
> *Alike at work and prayer*
> *To Jesus I repair;*
> *May Jesus Christ be praised.*

Rising Woe

MORNING SCRIPTURE   Isaiah 5:2-30
MORNING VERSE   Isaiah 5:11
Woe unto them that rise up early in the morning, that they may
follow strong drink; that continue until night, till wine inflame
them!

I n all His wisdom, Solomon posed no greater questions than
these: "Who hath woe? Who hath sorrow? Who hath contentions? Who hath babbling? Who hath wounds without
cause? Who hath redness of eyes?" (Proverbs 23:29). For the
answer to each of these questions Solomon continues, "They
that tarry long at the wine; they that go to seek mixed wine."

We must wonder why so many are given to wine and other
strong drink when drunkenness has produced such misery in
the lives of humanity. The result of drinking too much wine is
always woe, sorrow, contention, babbling, wounds without
cause, and redness of eyes. Nonetheless, our society is portrayed
as one in which social drinking at best and drunkenness at worst
are acceptable habits.

Concern for the adverse effects of alcohol has been reflected in the writings of men since the fermentation of the first grape.
The Bible writers frequently address themselves to this problem. Isaiah, the son of Amoz, and the most notable of the prophets, thought the subject worthy of his attention.

Having been born in Jerusalem, probably of noble parent-
age, Isaiah was the younger contemporary of Amos and Hosea,
prophets to the northern kingdom. He is said to have prophesied in the reigns of four kings of Judah: Uzziah, Jotham, Ahaz,
and Hezekiah (Isaiah 1:1). As a writer, Isaiah is superb. For
versatility of expression and brilliance of imagery there is no
one superior to him among the Hebrew authors. He is an artist,
painting pictures with words. Even Jerome likened the oratory
of Isaiah to that of Demosthenes.

Spending long hours during the day drinking wine has been
depicted as a sign of nobility and brilliance, if not great wealth
and sociability. If anyone in the Old Testament is an example of

nobility and sociability it is Isaiah. Still, this prophet of God expressed deep concern over those whose eyes are reddened with wine and whose tongues are given to babbling because of it. He says, "Woe unto them *that rise up early in the morning*, that they may follow strong drink; that continue until night, till wine inflame them!" (Isaiah 5 :11) Of all the activities to which man could give himself from early morning until the evening, Isaiah sees as one of the most detrimental rising early in the morning to begin a daylong bout with the bottle.

It appears that Isaiah's concern goes far beyond that of mere woe, sorrow, contentions, and babbling. Not that these are not sources of concern; they are. But when one rises early in the morning to follow strong drink all the day long, it keeps that person from a more noble pursuit, namely the pursuit of service for the Lord God. Isaiah continues in the next verse, "But they regard not the work of the LORD, neither consider the operation of His hands." When our minds are dulled by the influences of wine, when our eyes redden and our tongues thicken, we can no longer think clearly on the words of the Lord, nor can we see clearly the works of His hands, nor can we speak clearly of His saving grace to a dying world. In short, rising early to follow strong drink is entirely incompatible with rising early to seek the Lord.

It is little wonder, therefore, that Paul instructs the Ephesian believers, "Wherefore be ye not unwise, but understanding what the will of the Lord is. And be not drunk with wine, wherein is excess; but be filled with the Spirit; speaking to yourself in psalms and hymns and spiritual songs, singing and making melody in your heart to the Lord" (Ephesians 5:17-19). Let us rise early to be filled with the Spirit of God for a day of service and praise to Him. May God deliver us today from anything that would keep us from regarding the work of the Lord or considering the operations of His hand.

MORNING HYMN
> *Let my hands perform His bidding,*
> *Let my feet run in His ways;*
> *Let my eyes see Jesus only,*
> *Let my lips speak forth His praise.*

The Habit of Prayer

MORNING SCRIPTURE   Mark 1:16-39
MORNING VERSE   Mark 1:35
And in the morning, rising up a great while before day, He went out, and departed into a solitary place, and there prayed.

As the Lord Jesus walked along the shores of Galilee He encountered two fishermen, Peter and his brother Andrew. He called them to leave their nets, follow Him, and become fishers of men. Soon He encountered the sons of Zebedee, James and John, and they too followed the Master.

Jesus then entered the city of Capernaum on the Sabbath day and began to teach in the synagogue. Among those who listened to Jesus' teaching was a man with an unclean spirit. Jesus rebuked the spirit and commanded it to come out of the man. When Jesus and His followers left the synagogue they entered into the house of Peter and Andrew. Peter's mother-in-law was sick and near death when Jesus took her hand, lifted her up, and her fever immediately left her. As if that weren't enough for one day's work, that evening when the sun had set the multitudes brought unto Jesus all that were diseased and possessed with devils. It had been an exhausting day when Jesus pillowed His head that night, but one filled with convincing demonstrations of the power of God.

You would expect that after such a tiring but fruitful day, the Master would take His leave to sleep in the next morning. Instead of a little extra repose after a day of labor, however, Jesus rose up long before the dawn, *rising up a great while before day* (Mark 1:35). The Master rose up early to seek a solitary place to pray. As tired as He must have been, the Lord would allow nothing to interfere with His practice of rising early and praying alone.

It's good for us to get in the habit of prayer. We may pray about big things or about little things, but we must be in the habit of taking everything to the Lord in prayer. This was the habit of our Lord Jesus, as is evidenced by His early morning rendezvous with God the Father after a particularly trying day.

Being in the habit of prayer not only pleases God but it benefits us tremendously.

The story is told of a soldier who was brought before his commanding officer and accused of betraying his country by communicating with the enemy. The soldier had been seen emerging from an area where the enemy troops were known to hide out. When the young soldier was brought to trial he summed up his defense in just a few words, stating that he had slipped away to spend an hour alone in prayer. The officer, acting as prosecuting attorney, snapped at the young man, "Have you been in the habit of spending an hour in private prayer?"

"Yes sir," the young officer replied.

"Then," his commander retorted, "never in your life have you been in more need of prayer than now. Kneel down and pray aloud so we all may hear you."

Although the commander was being cynical and did not expect a response, the soldier dropped to his knees and poured out his heart to God. Immediately an intimacy with the heavenly Father was evident. His earnestness, his fluency, and his implicit trust that God would deliver him, unmistakably proved to the court that this soldier came regularly to the throne of grace.

"You may go," said the officer. "No one could have prayed that way without a long apprenticeship; the fellows who have never attended drill are always ill at ease for the review."

Covenant with God that you will rise early in the morning to seek His face in prayer. You won't believe the difference in how your day goes.

MORNING HYMN
> *I come to the garden alone,*
> *While the dew is still on the roses*
> *And the voice I hear,*
> *Falling on my ear,*
> *The Son of God discloses.*

Getting Ahead of God

MORNING SCRIPTURE   Genesis 21:1-21
MORNING VERSE   Genesis 21:14

And Abraham rose up early in the morning, and took bread, and a bottle of water, and gave it unto Hagar, putting it on her shoulder, and the child, and sent her away: and she departed, and wandered in the wilderness of Beer-sheba.

I t is sometimes disconcerting to board an airplane at the scheduled departure time and then have to endure a lengthy wait on the runway before being cleared for takeoff. Not only do you miss your appointments in a distant city, but you begin to wonder if the marvels of our space-age technology are so marvelous. Yet just as bad as an unscheduled delay would be an unscheduled hastening of the takeoff. You can imagine the turmoil if a flight scheduled for 2:00 o'clock departure left at 1:30. Getting ahead of what is designed can be just as devastating as falling behind.

Abraham was a great man of faith, a friend of God. When God called him to leave his homeland and go to an unknown destination, Abraham immediately obeyed. Later the Lord promised Abraham that his seed would be as numberless as the dust of the earth. But Abraham remained childless. His only heir was Eliezer of Damascus, whom he had adopted. When he questioned God, Abraham was told, "This shall not be thine heir; but he that shall come forth out of thine own loins shall be thine heir. And He brought him forth abroad, and said, Look now toward heaven, and count the stars, if thou be able to number them: and He said unto him, So shall they seed be." Abraham believed this promise and the Lord counted it to him for righteousness (Genesis 15:4-6).

Yet Abraham and his wife suffered from the same frailties all humans do. After years of expectation and disappointment, they began to wonder if the divine promise was really true. Barren Sarah decided to take matters into her own hands. She had an Egyptian handmaid whose name was Hagar. Herself not able to conceive, Sarah convinced Abraham to take Hagar as his wife so that she might bear him a son.

Although this was a common practice in the Ancient Near

East, nevertheless it was not the fulfillment of God's promise. The appointed time for the birth of Abraham's heir had not yet arrived, but Sarah wanted to force the issue. Shortly Abraham was presented with a son, but by Hagar, not Sarah. An angel of the Lord had previously instructed Hagar to name the child Ishmael. But the heavenly messenger also warned that the child would be a wild man and every man's hand would be against him.

It wasn't until twenty-four years later that the Lord performed a miracle for Sarah and the son of promise was born. Although Abraham was now one hundred years old, this was the promised time and Isaac was the promised son. On the eighth day Isaac was circumcised and months later Abraham made a great feast when the child was weaned. At this festive occasion the behavior of Ishmael betrayed his jealousy. He taunted his young half brother, mocked and ridiculed baby Isaac. As Sarah viewed this it raised her motherly dander. She demanded of her husband, "Cast out this bondwoman and her son; for the son of this bondwoman shall not be heir with my son, even with Isaac" (Genesis 21:10).

This grieved Abraham very much for Ishmael was his own flesh and blood. But God comforted him assuring him that, although Isaac was indeed the promised seed, nevertheless God would also make of Ishmael a great nation. Thus, "Abraham *rose up early in the morning,* and took bread, and a bottle of water," and bid Hagar and the boy a sad good-bye (Genesis 21:14).

God was kind to Ishmael and providentially protected his mother and him. But it was clear that Isaac was the child of promise, not Ishmael. Ishmael was the result of the impatience of Abraham and Sarah. The wild man was born because this couple got ahead of God. They believed that God would provide the promised seed but mistakenly attempted to speed up God's timetable. God performs what He promises, but always in His own time. "Wait on the LORD be of good courage, and He shall strengthen thine heart. Wait, I say, on the LORD" (Psalm 27:14). That's good advice for us today.

MORNING HYMN
> *My Jesus, as Thou wilt! O may Thy will be mine;*
> *Into Thy hand of love I would my all resign.*
> *Thro' sorrow, or thro' joy, Conduct me as Thine own;*
> *And help me still to say, My Lord, Thy will be done.*

Sin in the Camp

MORNING SCRIPTURE   Joshua 7:1-26
MORNING VERSE   Joshua 7:16
*So Joshua rose up early in the morning, and brought Israel by
their tribes; and the tribe of Judah was taken.*

Israel had just won the biggest battle in its military history. The impregnable fortress of Jericho was destroyed by the mighty hand of God. The inhabitants of Canaan trembled in terror before the armies of Israel. But as is frequently the case, a great victory had made them susceptible to a great defeat.

With the ashes of Jericho behind it, Israel now faced the next battle in its conquest of Canaan. Situated east of Bethel, in the foothills of the Judean highlands, was the tiny town of Ai. When spies returned from scouting this town they reported that only three thousand soldiers were needed to seize this tiny, indefensible town. What they did not know was that, whereas God had gone with them into battle at Jericho, because of sin in their ranks God would not go with them in battle at Ai. The Israelites soon learned that the difference between victory and defeat is not military strength but the presence of the Lord.

The men of Ai routed the Israelite force, slaying thirty-six of them and chasing the rest all the way to Shebarim. Licking their wounds, they returned to Joshua and the elders who immediately fell on their faces before the ark of the Lord. Joshua thought he had been abandoned by God, but the Lord quickly revealed to him that the defeat at Ai was due to sin in the camp of Israel. "So Joshua *rose up early in the morning*, and brought Israel by their tribes" (Joshua 7:16). The tribe of Judah was indicated. Then all the families of Judah were marched before Joshua and Zerah was pointed out as head of the sinning family. From the family of the Zerahites, man by man, they were escorted into the presence of Joshua and Zabdi was taken. The household of Zabdi remained and Achan, the son of Carmi, was accused.

Joshua bade Achan to give glory to the Lord God of Israel and make a public confession. Achan confessed that his sin began innocently enough when he saw the spoils of war. But immediately that simple sight degenerated into coveteousness and

51

to actually taking the accursed thing. But worse than that, because he thought he could get away with his sin, he hid the beautiful garment and the silver and gold he took in the earth beneath his tent. Although succumbing to the temptation to sin was evil enough, Achan's greatest mistake was thinking that he could hide that sin from God.

That we can never successfully hide our sin from God is the teaching of Jesus' parable of the lighted candle. Luke 8:16-17 records, "No man, when he hath lighted a candle, covereth it with a vessel, or putteth it under a bed; but setteth it on a candlestick, that they which enter in may see the light. For nothing is secret, that shall not be made manifest; neither anything hid, that shall not be made known and come abroad." The seeing eye of God searches even the innermost secrets of men. No sin, however large or small, escapes the eye of God.

Exodus 2 describes how Moses spied an Egyptian smiting a Hebrew, and he looked this way and that way, and when he saw no man watching him he slew the Egyptian and hid him in the sand (Exodus 2:12). The very next day however Moses' sin was discovered and he had to flee from the land of the Pharaoh and spend the next forty years in Midian. Moses' sin was unsuccessfully hidden. Beloved King David had a similar experience. After sinning with Bathsheba and attempting to cover his sin through the death of Uriah the Hittite, the trespass of David soon came to light when Nathan the prophet pointed his finger in the king's face and said, "Thou art the man" (2 Samuel 12:7). In remorse King David said, "O God, Thou knowest my foolishness; and my sins are not hid from Thee" (Psalm 69:5).

From the sad experiences of Achan and these others, let us learn well the truth that sin is never successfully hidden. We cannot hide our sin from God; we only can deal with it. "If we confess our sins, he is faithful and just to forgive us our sins, and to cleanse us from all unrighteousness" (1 John 1:9). Don't try to hide sin today; let God forgive it instead.

MORNING HYMN

> *Depth of mercy! can there be*
> *Mercy still reserved for me?*
> *Can my Cod His wrath forbear*
> *Me, the chief of sinners spare?*

Love and Patience

MORNING SCRIPTURE   Jeremiah 7:1-34
MORNING VERSE   Jeremiah 7:25
Since the day that your fathers came forth out of the land of Egypt unto this day I have even sent unto you all My servants the prophets, daily rising up early and sending them.

There is no greater contrast in all the Bible than the love and patience of God with the general disregard for that love and patience by men. Perhaps this theme is more clearly seen in the prophecy of Jeremiah than in any other.

Jeremiah is one of the most colorful figures in Hebrew history. This is undoubtedly due to the fact that we know more about his personality and character than we do about any other of the Old Testament prophets. Called of God when he was but a child (Jeremiah 1:6), Jeremiah knew personally the love and patience of God and prophesied for Jehovah for nearly half a century. His concern was to bring Israel back to God in repentance and faith. Tragically, he stood in the mainstream of an ungrateful people who were rushing to certain destruction, yet they sought not God.

Jehovah was so concerned for His people that He commissioned Jeremiah to "stand in the gate of the LORD's house, and proclaim there this word, and say, Hear the word of the LORD, all ye of Judah, that enter in at these gates to worship the LORD" (Jeremiah 7:2). God would not permit His people to face imminent destruction and death without the opportunity to repent and be restored. Jeremiah's task was to stand between the Jews and certain destruction.

In a delightful picture of the concern of Jehovah for His people, Jeremiah 7 twice indicates that God did not simply commission the prophet and then withdraw Himself from interest in the Jews. Jeremiah 7:13 says, "And now, because ye have done all these works, saith the LORD, and I spake unto you, *rising up early* and speaking but ye heard not; and I called you, but ye answered not." It is natural for anyone who has loved ones facing impending danger to show diligence in dealing with it. The same is true for Jehovah God. It is no impassive God who is seen here. God takes a profound interest in His people. This anthropomorphic expression indicates that God is not disengaged from His people or the affairs that affect them. He mourns over their sin and rejoices in their salvation. Still they do not heed His call for repentance and thus He must deliver them into the hand of the enemy.

The expression of Jehovah's rising early is strengthened in verse 25. Here He reminds His people, "Since the day that your fathers came forth out of the land of Egypt unto this day I have even sent unto you all My servants the prophets, *daily rising up early* and sending them." It is not the prophets alone who are said to rise early with the message of repentance, but God Himself. Day after day, He rises to recommission anew these prophets with their life-changing message.

And what will be Israel's response to this consistent love and concern of Jehovah? Joshua 7:26 indicates, "Yet they hearkened not unto Me, nor inclined their ear, but hardened their neck; they did worse than their fathers." What a contrast! God calls and commissions prophets to bring His message to a wayward people. He rises early every morning and sends forth His prophets. Still, day after day, His people do not hearken unto Him but harden their necks and become even more stubborn in their sin.

Today God is just as concerned about us as He was about Old Testament Israel. He showers His mercy on us as He did on them. He warns us of our sin as He warned the Jews. And much like them, we do not listen, nor do we heed the warnings of those whom He has raised to call us to repentance. Remember, before we arose early to seek God today, He had already risen to prepare this day for us. In response to His great love and concern for us, let us serve Him faithfully today.

MORNING HYMN
> *Love divine, all loves excelling,*
> *Joy of heav'n to earth come down;*
> *Fix in us Thy humble dwelling,*
> *All Thy faithful mercies crown.*
> *Jesus, Thou art all compassion,*
> *Pure, unbounded love Thou art;*
> *Visit us with Thy salvation,*
> *Enter ev'ry trembling heart.*

Christ Our Anchor

MORNING SCRIPTURE   2 Kings 3:1-27
MORNING VERSE   2 Kings 3:22
*And they rose up early in the morning, and the sun shone upon
the water, and the Moabites saw the water on the other side as red
as blood.*

After the death of Solomon the empire of Israel was
sharply divided. The ten tribes to the north comprised
the northern kingdom; the two tribes to the south formed
the southern kingdom. For the most part, the kings of the south
were a mixture of good and bad. Without exception, the Jewish
kings of Israel, the ten tribes to the north, were all bad. In 2
Kings 3 is the story of a northern Jewish king who failed to call
on God and a southern Jewish king who remembered to call on
God.

The defeat of Ahab at Ramoth, and the subsequent domin-
ion of the Assyrians over the territory east of the Jordan, encouraged the king of Moab to revolt against Israel. Mesha refused to
pay his annual tribute of one hundred lambs and one hundred
thousand rams. The scriptural account of this revolt receives
absolute confirmation from the Moabite Stone, discovered in
1868 and now reconstructed at the Louvre Museum in Paris.
Jehoram, the king of Israel, sought help from Jehoshaphat, the
king of Judah, to march against Mesha of Moab in retaliation
for his rebellion. Jehoshaphat agreed. They planned to enter
Moab by way of the wilderness of Edom. The king of Edom, a
vassal of Judah, joined the expedition.

After a seven-day march through the desert, the armies of
the Jews and Edomites were without water. They would soon
die if something was not done. Jehoshaphat, who wished to
consult a prophet of Jehovah, soon learned that Elisha was in
the camp of Israel. Elisha told them to dig trenches over the
plains and promised that God would both fill them with water
and give a complete victory over Moab. This they did throughout the night in order to prepare for God's divine provision of
water in the morning.

When the enemy armies of the Moabites rose up early in the morning, the red rays of the rising sun reflected from the waters that God had miraculously sent to fill the Jewish trenches (2 Kings 3:22). The Moabites misinterpreted the red hue of the water to be a lake of blood. They assumed that the allied armies had turned on each other and destroyed themselves. Thus the Moabite armies charged out of their camp to help themselves to the supposed spoils of war.

Rushing in disorder upon the Israelite camp, they were met by the whole army of the Jews and pushed back into their own country. The cities of Moab were razed, stones were thrown into the fields, wells were filled, and fruit trees were cut down. A great deliverance was given to Israel and to Judah because one king, Jehoshaphat, had not failed to seek help from Jehovah. In the midst of a disastrous situation he remembered the words of his forefather David, "In Thee, O Lord, do I put my trust" (Psalm 71:1).

"Can you imagine the captain of a ship, driven about by rough winds and desiring to drop anchor, trying to find a suitable place on board his own vessel? Such a thing seems ridiculous. He hangs the anchor at the prow, but still the boat drives before the wind; he casts it upon the deck but this too fails to hold it steady; at last he puts it down into the hold but has no better success. You see, an anchor resting on the storm-driven craft itself will never do the job. Only as it is thrown into the deep can it be effective against wind and tide. In the very same way, that person whose confidence is in himself will never experience true peace and safety. His actions are as futile as one who seeks to keep the anchor aboard his own ship. So cast your faith into the great depths of God's eternal love and power" (author unknown).

Although Jehoram would have been content to go into battle alone, Jehoshaphat would find contentment only in dropping his anchor in the love and wisdom of Jehovah. Let's not settle for less today.

MORNING HYMN
Will your anchor hold in the storms of life,
When the clouds unfold their wings of strife?
When the strong tides lift and the cables strain,
Will your anchor drift or firm remain?

God's Compassion

MORNING SCRIPTURE   Jonah 1:1-4:11
MORNING VERSE   Jonah 4:7
*But God prepared a worm when the morning rose the next day,
and it smote the gourd that it withered.*

T he story of Jonah is told in four short chapters, each chapter containing snapshots of Jonah and lessons that we should learn from his life. The purpose of the book is made clear by reading through its chapters as one would a photo album. Let's notice the twelve snapshots of Jonah in this scrapbook of his life.

Snapshot one is *Jonah the Sinner*. The word of the Lord had come to Jonah and instructed him clearly to arise, go to Nineveh, and cry out against it. But Jonah the sinner instead "rose up to flee unto Tarshish from the presence of the LORD" (1:3).

Snapshot two is *Jonah the Sleeper*. Shortly after his ship sailed, a violent storm erupted. Jonah was asleep in the hold of the ship (1:6), much like Jesus on a similar occasion in Mark 4:38. But whereas Jonah slept, thinking he had escaped from the hand of God, Jesus slept knowing He was safe in the hand of God.

Snapshot three is *Jonah the Salvager*. As the storm continued the men in the boat threw the cargo overboard to lighten the vessel. Jonah, who now confessed his guilt, directed the mariners to cast him into the sea in an attempt to salvage the ship (1:12).

Snapshot four is *Jonah the Swimmer*. Having taken up Jonah and cast him into the sea, the winds and seas ceased from their raging (1:15). The mariners saw the power of Jonah's God and when they saw the great fish swallow Jonah they feared Jehovah even more.

Snapshot five is *Jonah the Supplicator*. From out of the fish's belly Jonah began to pray in earnest to the Lord (2:1). In his darkest hour and at the point of his greatest need, Jonah had not forgotten how to get hold of God.

Snapshot six is *Jonah the Soul-searcher*. In the belly of the great fish, with the contents of the fish's stomach entwined around him, Jonah had ample opportunity to search his own soul and see the root cause of God's judgment on him (2:5).

Snapshot seven is *Jonah the Surrenderer*. In this most unlikely place, Jonah surrendered to the Lord. In the belly of the great fish Jonah learned his greatest theological lesson, that "salvation is of the LORD" (2:9). He got a good dose of "whale belly theology."

Snapshot eight is *Jonah the Second-chancer*. The God of the second chance spoke the word of the Lord unto Jonah a second time and recommissioned him to preach at Nineveh (3:1-2). Jonah thought he had resigned his commission; God simply reassigned that commission.

Snapshot nine is *Jonah the Submitter*. This time Jonah could not wait to travel to the city of Nineveh in order to fulfill God's commission (3:3). He submitted to the will of God and immediately trekked to the great city of Nineveh.

Snapshot ten is *Jonah the Succeeder*. When Jonah entered Nineveh and began to preach his message of salvation (3:5), the people believed God and repented of their sins. Jonah's mission had been entirely successful.

Snapshot eleven is *Jonah the Second-guesser*. No sooner had Jonah finished his great task of winning the lost to the Lord than it displeased him exceedingly (4:1). As a Jew sent to the enemy Assyrian nation, Jonah could not understand how God could show mercy to the wicked Ninevites. Who can second guess the purpose of God (cf. Hebrews 11:32-38, Ephesians 1:4-5,9; Isaiah 46:10)?

Snapshot twelve is *Jonah the Sulker*. So distraught was Jonah that he sat in a hastily prepared booth and sulked. Here God prepared a gourd to grow up over Jonah for shadow from the sun. But "when *the morning rose the next day*" God also prepared a worm to eat the gourd and wither away the vine (Jonah 4:7).

God's infinite compassion for humanity, regardless of race or color, and our duty under God to convey the news of His salvation to every land, is the lesson we must learn from the prophecy of Jonah. God's mercy in salvation extends far beyond us; His mercy extends to the entire world.

MORNING HYMN
> *There is welcome for the sinner*
> *And more graces for the good;*
> *There is mercy with the Saviour,*
> *There is healing in His blood.*

Mercy Amid Judgment

MORNING SCRIPTURE   Exodus 9:13-35
MORNING VERSE   Exodus 9:13
*And the LORD said unto Moses, Rise up early in the morning,
and stand before Pharaoh, and say unto him, Thus saith the LORD
God of the Hebrews, Let My people go, that they may serve Me.*

One of the great paradoxes of the Bible is God's compassionate practice of tempering judgment with mercy. If ever anyone deserved the biting edge of God's wrath, it was the Pharaoh of the exodus. He was cruel, vindictive, and hard-hearted. When Moses and Aaron appeared before him, seeking the release of the Israelites, Pharaoh was insolent and blasphemous. He deserved to be stricken by God, yet he was spared through the plagues of blood, frogs, lice, flies, malignant livestock, and boils.

Now once again the Lord instructed Moses to *"rise up early in the morning* and stand before Pharaoh, and say unto him, Thus saith the LORD God of the Hebrews, Let My people go' (Exodus 9:13). Yet another plague was to be inflicted on the Egyptians unless their king abandoned his insane rebellion against the Lord God. The first six plagues were accompanied by much suffering and humiliation. However, none of these had actually touched the lives of the Egyptians. This time, if Pharaoh did not relent, God would smite the people and their land with pestilence and they would be cut off from the earth.

Characteristic of God's mercy, the pestilence was not to begin immediately. Moses predicted, "Behold, tomorrow about this time I will cause it to rain a very grievous hail, such as hath not been in Egypt since the foundation thereof even until now.' God gave the Egyptian king time for reflection. Judgment was impending, but before it came the mercy of God allowed the rebellious Pharaoh twenty-four hours to consider the folly of his resistance.

But God's mercy did not stop there. Every God-fearing Egyptian had opportunity to respond to God as well. Those servants of Pharaoh who feared the word of the Lord, probably as a result of the previous plagues, quickly sought shelter for their families and cattle. Those who regarded not the word of the Lord remained in the fields.

Wherever the word of God is heralded the reaction is always the same. Some believe and receive; others ridicule and reject. When the Apostle Paul delivered his compelling address on Mars' Hill some mocked, others delayed, and a few believed (Acts 17:32-34). Nowhere is this more emphatically stated than in the final chapter of the Acts. "And some believed the things which were spoken, and some believed not" (Acts 28:24).

When the period of reflection and response was over, judgment came as promised. The thunder cracked, and the Lord sent hail and fire on the land of Egypt. So fierce was the hail and fire that upon impact great balls of fire ran along the ground. This pestilence smote both man and beast in the fields as well as the herbs and trees throughout Egypt. Yet the land of Goshen, where the people of God resided, was not touched. Neither were the Egyptians who had heeded the word of the Lord and took shelter—another instance of God's mercy, even during judgment.

Perhaps the greatest example of God's mercy in the midst of judgment is seen after the plague. Since many Egyptians had lost their lives, Pharaoh made a halfhearted, mock repentance in order to stay the mighty thunderings and hail. The flax and barley crops were completely destroyed for the barley was in ear and the flax in bud. But the wheat and rye crops were yet in the ground and not destroyed. Those Egyptians who remained were not left without the hope of a harvest. That's the mercy of God!

Though Pharaoh's rebellion and insolence deserved the utter destruction of God's judgment, yet before, during, and after the plague of hail the mercy of God is evident. God's pity rests on men who have none on themselves. "The LORD is gracious, and full of compassion, slow to anger, and of great mercy. The LORD is good to all, and His tender mercies are over all His works" (Psalm 145:8-9). Let's thank Him today for His great mercy.

MORNING HYMN

> *There's a wideness in God's mercy,*
> *Like the wideness of the sea*
> *There's a kindness in His justice,*
> *Which is more than liberty.*

Working Together

MORNING SCRIPTURE   Nehemiah 4:1-23
MORNING VERSE   Nehemiah 4:21
So we labored in the work; and half of them held the spears from the rising of the morning till the stars appeared.

It was not until the year 539 B.C. that the Persian king Cyrus decreed that Jews and other captives could return to their homelands after a long Babylonian captivity. Wave after wave of expatriates made the journey back to a beleaguered land of promise. While yet captive, however, the news came to Nehemiah that the wall of Jerusalem had never been repaired since its destruction by Nebuchadnezzar. Brigands and robbers could attack the city at will. Nehemiah was distressed and became terribly burdened for his home town. He secured the necessary papers from Artaxerxes, the Persian king at that time, to return to his homeland and rebuild the wall around Jerusalem.

In 444 B.C. Nehemiah arrived in Jerusalem and soon afterwards went by night on an inspection tour of the city walls. He elicited help to rebuild the ruined fortification both from residents and returnees. Volunteers quickly came to his side, but so did villains. Sanballat the Horonite and Tobiah the Ammonite heard that Nehemiah had come to rebuild the walls and "it grieved them exceedingly that there was a man come to seek the welfare of the children of Israel" (Nehemiah 2:10).

At first Sanballat and Tobiah had only scorned the idea that these feeble Jews would fortify their city. But now they had become seriously alarmed. A conspiracy was formed of the Arabians, Ammonites, and Philistines of Ashdod. The enemies of Nehemiah were ready to attack Jerusalem before the fortifications could be completed.

When Nehemiah heard the news of this conspiracy he made the proper response. Nehemiah 4:9 says, "Nevertheless, we made our prayer unto our God, and set a watch against them day and night, because of them." Nehemiah immediately turned to God in prayer but just as immediately made preparations to defend himself. This is the delicate balance between faith and works which is needed in each of our lives. With a trowel in one hand and a sword in the other the workmen continued to rebuild the walls. They would both watch and pray. The end result was summed up in Nehemiah's words, "So we labored in the work: and half of them held the spears from the rising of the morning till the stars appeared" (Nehemiah 4:21). With each one doing his part, the task was finished in record time to the glory of the Lord.

The story could have been much different if, for example those who worked complained that those who watched were not doing their fair share. Nehemiah's workmen had to recognize they were all laborers together with God (1 Corinthians 3:9), as we must today if we are going to accomplish anything for God

The following parable illustrates this principle. A carpenter's tools were having a conference. Brother Hammer was presiding, but the others informed him that he'd have to leave because he was too noisy. "All right," he said, "I'll go, but Brother Plane must withdraw too, there's no depth to his work. It's always on the surface." Brother Plane responded, "Well, Brother Rule will also have to go. He's constantly measuring people as if he were the only one who's right." Brother Rule complained about Brother Sandpaper saying, "He's always rubbing people the wrong way." In the midst of the discussion the Carpenter of Nazareth entered. He went to His workbench to make a pulpit from which He would preach the gospel. He used the hammer, the plane, the rule, and the sandpaper. All were important in their own way.

If Christians criticize one another, insult one another, and refuse to work together for God, the task of gleaning the whitened harvest fields will never be completed for His glory. Though differences remain between believers, let us always recognize who the true enemy really is. It is Satan. Each of us possesses different gifts and abilities, but none of us is unimportant in the work of the Lord. Let's defeat our common enemy this day.

MORNING HYMN
> *To the work! to the work! we are servants of God,*
> *Let us follow the path that our Master has trod;*
> *With the balm of His counsel our strength to renew,*
> *Let us do with our might what our hands find to do.*

Giving Thanks

MORNING SCRIPTURE   Psalm 92:1-15
MORNING VERSE   Psalm 92:2
To shew forth Thy loving-kindness in the morning, and Thy faithfulness every night.

Some years ago a man attended the services of a Chicago rescue mission. The man radiated Christian joy. You could see the love of the Lord Jesus all over his face. He had few possessions and very little money, but his smile was that of a man who owned the world.

One day he entered the mission with a bandage on his thumb. When questioned what had happened, he explained that he had smashed his thumb with a hammer. Immediately he added, "But praise the Lord. I still have my thumb!" Later, he scraped together what little money he had to purchase some groceries. On his way home he noticed that his shoelace had become untied. Setting the package off to one side while he tied his shoe, a large dog came on the scene, sniffed at the contents of the bag, and made off with it. Later, he recounted this experience with characteristic cheerfulness, "Praise the Lord. I still have my appetite left!" He always found reasons to be grateful.

Today many are skeptical of people who have this attitude toward life. They say that these people are too simplistic, that they do not have a firm grasp on reality. The unsaved man does not understand how a believer could thank God for such bitter things in the face of want.

Those who have not experienced the grace of God in salvation cannot appreciate the truth of our psalm today. The psalmist begins with the exclamation, "It is a good thing to give thanks unto the LORD." There are no qualifying clauses to this statement. The psalmist does not say it is right to praise the Lord when things are going our way. He does not say we are to give thanks when there is food on the table and money in the bank. Without any reservation at all, the psalmist simply states that it is good to give thanks unto the Lord.

Why does he make such a statement? It is good to give

thanks unto the Lord because it is good *ethically*, for it is the Lord's right. The Lord is gracious, therefore to give thanks unto Him is good. It is also good *emotionally* to thank the Lord. It brings pleasure to the heart of the one who offers the sacrifice of praise to God. As well, it is good *practically* to give thanks unto the Lord for it will inspire others to do the same. To give thanks to God is small return for the great benefits He bestows upon us daily.

In addition to this, the psalmist continues, "And to sing praises unto Thy name, O Most High." Silent worship is sweet, but vocal worship is sweeter. We must never deny our tongues the privilege of praising God. Nature itself teaches us to express our gratitude to God in this way. Do not the birds sing? Do not the brooks warble as they flow? Why then should not our tongues give rise to a song of praise unto God?

The psalmist even teaches us when to sing our song of praise unto God: "To show forth Thy loving-kindness *in the morning*" (Psalm 92:2). No hour of the day is too early for a song of praise unto God. In fact, praise for His loving-kindness toward us is most appropriate during those dewy hours when morning catches its first glimpse of the oriental sun caressing the earth. There is a freshness and charm about early morning praises that cannot be matched at any other hour of the day. Praise the Lord early and we will praise Him well.

No matter how skeptical others may be of our unusual spirit of gratitude toward God, like the man who attended the services at the Chicago rescue mission, let us always find reason to give thanks unto Him. Morning, noon, and night our voices should be raised in a song of praise to the one who alone is worthy of our praise.

MORNING HYMN

Praise ye the Lord!
O let all that is in me adore Him!
All that hath life and breath,
Come now with praises before Him!
Let the Amen sound from His people again:
Gladly for aye we adore Him.

Obedience

MORNING SCRIPTURE   Genesis 22:1-14
MORNING VERSE   Genesis 22:3
And Abraham rose up early in the morning, and saddled his ass, and took two of his young men with him, and Isaac his son, and clave the wood for the burnt offering, and rose up, and went unto the place of which God had told him.

Obedience to God's call is the prerequisite to God's blessing. If we are not willing to relinquish our own interests in compliance with God's call to duty, we should not expect His blessing automatically to be ours. To Abraham the Lord promised, "I will make of thee a great nation, and I will bless thee, and make thy name great; and thou shalt be a blessing" (Genesis 12:2). Before these promises were realized, however, the patriarch had to prove his absolute obedience unto God.

Four times Abraham endured the test of obedience and each time it was related to separation. Initially he received the divine call to leave kindred and country behind and journey to an unknown land. Later he found his nephew's herdsmen at odds with his own and Abraham had to separate himself once more from his kin. Still later this obedient servant of God found his wife Sarah engaged in a jealous battle with her handmaid and Abraham had to bid a sad good-bye to Hagar and his young son of the flesh, Ishmael. Each of these events tested Abraham's obedience to God and each was passed with flying colors.

However, Abraham was yet to undergo a final test of loyalty. This was to be the fourth and supreme test of separation. The Lord said, "Take now thy son, thine only son Isaac, whom thou lovest, and get thee into the land of Moriah; and offer him there for a burnt offering upon one of the mountains which I will tell thee of" (Genesis 22:2).

Abraham's parents were long gone. Lot was gone. Ishmael was now gone. But as long as Isaac was alive, God's promise of blessing was yet intact. Now, however, was the son of promise to be sacrificed? Was he to be gone as well? You can well imagine the consternation in Abraham's heart. He had given up so much; must he give up his only son whom he loved? Reason told him no. But Abraham immediately brought his reason into the captivity of his faith. As soon as he received God's call to duty Abraham took no counsel with flesh and blood but rose early in the morning and set out with Isaac to the land of Moriah (Genesis 22:3). True obedience neither procrastinates nor questions.

The journey was upwards of sixty miles. On the third day Abraham bid the two young men accompanying them to remain behind with the donkey while he and his son went yonder to worship. Abraham grabbed the container of fire and a knife, while the wood for the burnt offering was laid upon the back of his only son, Isaac. How reminiscent this is of Abraham's greater son, the Lord Jesus Christ, who also bore the wood upon which He was sacrificed as a sin offering for us (John 19:17).

Once alone with his father, Isaac pointed out that they had fire and wood but no lamb for the sacrifice. In faith Abraham replied, "My son, God will provide Himself a lamb for a burnt offering" (Genesis 22:8). Yet as they came to Moriah, Abraham built an altar, laid the wood in order, and bound Isaac his only son, gently laying him on the altar. As he raised the knife to slay his son, Abraham must have spent an agonizing eternity with his hand in the air. Then suddenly the angel of the Lord called out to him, forbidding Isaac to be slain. A ram was provided and Abraham offered it as a burnt offering in place of his son. This totally unexpected ending to Abraham's personal ordeal prompted him to name that place Jehovah-jireh—the Lord will provide.

The supreme test was over. The Lord had not tempted Abraham with evil but rather provided a proving ground for his unflinching obedience. Now Abraham could indeed be the father of a great nation and be greatly blessed of the Lord. Like the patriarch, all who hear God's call to duty must tread the path of absolute obedience before we discover the many blessings along the way. "Blessed is every one that feareth the LORD, that walketh in His ways...happy shalt thou be, and it shall be well with thee" (Psalm 128:1-2).

MORNING HYMN
But we never can prove, The delights of His love
Until all on the altar we lay; For the favor He shows,
And the joy He bestows, Are for them who will trust and obey.

Jesus Our Passover

MORNING SCRIPTURE   Exodus 12:1-30
MORNING VERSE   Exodus 12:22
And ye shall take a bunch of hyssop, and dip it in the blood that is in the basin, and strike the lintel and the two side posts with the blood that is in the basin; and none of you shall go out at the door of his house until the morning.

At last the climax was at hand. After four hundred and thirty years of dwelling in Egypt, the Israelites were about to leave the land. Their oppressors had endured nine intense plagues; still the heart of Pharaoh was hardened. Moses warned the Egyptian ruler that if he did not let God's people go, the Lord would pass through the land and all the firstborn of Egypt would die. This was to be the final and most crushing judgment of all.

In preparation for this night, the Lord instructed Moses and Aaron to have each Israelite household separate a lamb from their flocks on the tenth day of the month. This was to be no ordinary lamb, but one without blemish. On the fourteenth day the Israelites would kill the lamb and strike its blood on the two side posts and upper doorpost of their houses. They were absolutely to remain inside their houses that night, for while Israel would be safely fellowshiping inside their blood-sprinkled houses, the firstborn of all outside would be killed. The Lord would "pass through" the land of Egypt at midnight but "pass over" those houses to which the lamb's blood was applied.

That the Passover celebration is an Old Testament type prefiguring Jesus Christ cannot be seriously questioned. The lamb was to be without blemish, publicly observed four days to make sure. The public life of our Lord proved He was without the blemish of sin (John 18:38). He was "the Lamb of God" (John 1:29), "without spot or blemish" (1 Peter 1:19), "holy, harmless, undefiled" (Hebrews 7:26). The lamb was to be slain in order that Israel might be saved from death. The blood of Jesus Christ was shed at Calvary in order that He might redeem us from death (Acts 20:28; Hebrews 9:12).

That Passover night was the fourteenth of the Jewish month Nisan or Abib (March/April). God instructed that "This month shall be unto you the beginning of months: it shall be the first month of the year to you" (Exodus 12:2). Because Israel was spared by the blood of the lamb, their future took on a new perspective. This was a new starting point in their existence. That night they began their journey to the promised land.

How this typifies the newness that salvation brings to a man's house! When we receive the atonement made for us by the blood of Jesus Christ, new life begins. We are "born again" (John 3:3); we are "passed from death unto life" (John 5:24); we are a "new creature" (2 Corinthians 5:17). The believer in Christ doesn't have a new lease on life; he has a new life entirely.

Exodus 12:22 summarizes the Passover instructions given to Israel. "And ye shall take a bunch of hyssop, and dip it in the blood that is in the basin, and strike the lintel and the two side posts with the blood that is in the basin; and none of you shall go out at the door of his house *until the morning.*" Even though the blood of the lamb was shed, it still was of no effect until it was applied to the house. So, too, the blood of Christ has no effect for us until it is applied to our lives (John 3:36). But once applied, all who are under the blood are spared from death and begin a journey to life eternal.

The Passover celebration became a perpetual memorial to God's deliverance of Israel. Many years later, as Christ and His disciples met for the Passover meal, He instituted the Lord's Supper which was to be partaken of in remembrance of His atoning death, the true Paschal Lamb. Paul reminds us, "For as often as ye eat this bread, and drink this cup, ye do show the Lord's death till He come" (1 Corinthians 11:26). Israel fellowshiped in their blood-stained houses until the morning. Let each of us remain in the fellowship of those who are bought with the blood of the Lamb, "until that bright and cloudless morning when the dead in Christ shall rise, and the glory of His resurrection share."

MORNING HYMN
> *What can wash away my sin?*
> *Nothing but the blood of Jesus;*
> *What can make me whole again?*
> *Nothing but the blood of Jesus.*

A Father's Failure

MORNING SCRIPTURE   1 Samuel 3:1-21
MORNING VERSE   1 Samuel 3:15
And Samuel lay until the morning, and opened the doors of the house of the LORD. And Samuel feared to show Eli the vision.

The Bible is filled with remarkable contrasts between people. For example, consider Samuel and the sons of Eli. Samuel, who was not Eli's son but was nurtured in the Lord by Eli, was a young man who found favor in the eyes of God. Hophni and Phinehas, who were Eli's sons but were not nurtured in the Lord by Eli, found nothing but shame in the eyes of God.

Born in answer to prayer and dedicated at birth by his mother to the service of the Lord, Samuel was trained at Shiloh by Eli the priest. His heart was tender toward the Lord and his ears were open to hear God's voice. Eli's sons were "sons of Belial" and instead of being content with that portion of the sacrifices allotted to them by law, they devised devious means of obtaining greater portions of the sacrifice. Moreover, they profaned the Tabernacle with their licentious practices at the very door of the house of God.

1 Samuel 3:13 correctly describes the attitude which led to the downfall of Hophni and Phinehas. Speaking of Eli's sons the Bible says, "His sons made themselves vile, and he restrained them not." Here is a classic case of a man so involved in his ministry that he neglected his family. Someone has said, perhaps with tongue in cheek, that if a man sees his sons going down the wrong track, probably it's because he did not switch them soon enough. Eli certainly failed to "switch" his sons and keep them on track for God.

During those days of crisis God had been strangely silent. "The word of the Lord was precious in those days; there was no open vision." But God decided to speak face to face with Samuel and in the middle of the night called out to him. The young child's immediate response was, "Here am I." Samuel ran to the bedside of Eli, assuming the voice was his. The priest sent him back to bed, perhaps thinking that the young lad was only dreaming. Twice again this strange phenomenon occurred and finally Eli recognized this to be the voice of God. His advice to Samuel was the next time the voice called to answer, "Speak LORD; for thy servant heareth." The boy returned to bed.

When the Lord called him again, Samuel answered as Eli had instructed, "And the LORD said to Samuel, Behold, I will do a thing in Israel, at which both the ears of every one that heareth it shall tingle." Jehovah was about to judge Eli and his family for their failure to heed His word and for the sons' unrighteousness at the temple door. Being the bearer of such information to one who had been both his mentor and friend would not be an easy task for Samuel. He *lay until the morning* awaiting God's courage (1 Samuel 3:15). When asked by Eli in the morning what the Lord spoke to him through the night, Samuel reluctantly imparted that information to the priest.

In the contrast between Samuel and Hophni and Phinehas it is worthy to note that while Hophni and Phinehas were born into their service, there is no evidence that they ever appreciated their position before the Lord. Samuel, on the other hand, was born outside of the service of God but was dedicated to it at birth. Had Eli "switched" his sons more often and instilled in them a reverence for the Lord, as he did Samuel, the ears of Israel would have had no occasion to tingle at the tragic deaths of Eli and his wicked sons (see 1 Samuel 4:10-22). Fathers, take care that you don't "gain the whole world but lose your own family."

MORNING HYMN
> *Take the world, but give me Jesus*
> *All its joys are but a name;*
> *But His love abideth ever*
> *Through eternal years the same.*

Unanswered Prayer

MORNING SCRIPTURE   Hosea 5:2-15
MORNING VERSE   Hosea 5:15
I will go and return to My place, till they acknowledge their offence, and seek My face: in their affliction they will seek Me early.

Hosea was a resident of the northern kingdom. Through out his prophecy it is evident that Hosea had a tender feeling of compassion for the people of his land.

Alternately he warned the people and then pled with them to return to God in repentance. He knew, regardless of how wicked they had been, if they repented of their sins and forsook their wicked ways, God would receive them back in His love.

In Hosea 5:2 the prophet described the Israelites as "the revolters" and himself as "a rebuker." He saw it as his task to point out Israel's sin and call them to repentance. But there was a problem. Of the Jews he said, "They shall go with their flocks and with their herds to seek the LORD; but they shall not find Him; He hath withdrawn Himself from them." God does not answer our prayers if we have unconfessed personal sin in our lives. Again and again the Bible affirms this truth (see John 9:31; Psalm 66:18; Isaiah 59:1-2).

We should not assume that God will always hear and answer our prayers. There are many things that can militate against God's answer. The greatest hindrance to answered prayer is personal, unconfessed sin. The Apostle Peter, after listing a variety of attitudes that a righteous person will have, makes this observation: "For the eyes of the Lord are over the righteous and His ears are open unto their prayers: but the face of the Lord is against them that do evil" (1 Peter 3:12). Many other things in life block the divine answer to prayer: idolatry (Jeremiah 11:11-14), irreverence for the Bible (Proverbs 28:7-9) family problems (1 Peter 3:1-7); improper motives (James 4:3), prayer without faith (James 1:5-6); but the most certain way to make God unavailable to us when we seek Him is for us to harbor iniquity in our hearts.

If the conditions were met, God would not withdraw Himself from Israel, He would listen to their prayers, and He would answer them. Therefore, Jehovah promised, "I will go and return to My place, till they acknowledge their offense and seek My face; in their affliction they will *seek Me early*" (Hosea 5:15). The absence of God's influence in their lives would be affliction enough for the Israelites. God was about to get their attention and He would do so by means of the calamities which Hosea prophesied. But once He got their attention and their repentance for sin was made, they would again arise early in the morning to seek the face of God.

If God appears to have withdrawn Himself from you, perhaps you ought to ask yourself these questions: "Have I treated God well enough for Him to answer my prayers?" (idolatry); "Have I heeded God's Word well enough for Him to answer my prayers?" (irreverence for the Bible); "Have I treated my family well enough for God to answer my prayers?" (family problems); "Have I examined my motives well enough for God to answer my prayers?" (improper motives); "Have I trusted God well enough for Him to answer my prayers?" (prayer without faith); "Have I confessed personal sin well enough for God to answer my prayers?" (iniquity). When we can answer each of these questions in the affirmative, there is no reason for God to withdraw Himself from us when we seek Him. He has promised always to be near. Having confessed our sin, let us claim that promise today.

MORNING HYMN
> *Power in prayer, Lord, power in prayer,*
> *Here 'mid earth's sin and sorrow and care;*
> *Men lost and dying, souls in despair—*
> *O give me power, power in prayer!*

God's Timetable

MORNING SCRIPTURE   Numbers 14:11-45
MORNING VERSE   Numbers 14:40
And they rose up early in the morning, and gat them up into the top of the mountain, saying, Lo, we be here, and will go up unto the place which the LORD hath promised: for we have sinned.

I f the child of God is to obey the will of God, he must keep his eye on the timetable of God. Israel had been miraculously delivered from Egyptian bondage by the evident power of God. Two months later the Israelites camped at the foot of Mount Sinai where Moses received the law of God. Here they remained nearly a year until God commanded them to move on to Kadesh-barnea. Everything was right on God's schedule.

God had led His people each step of the way. But before He would lead them into the promised land this luscious countryside had to be explored. For this task the twelve heads of their respective tribes were chosen. Their names are given at length but only two of them are memorable: Joshua the son of Nun, and Caleb the son of Jephunneh.

The twelve spies spent forty days on their intelligence gathering foray. Sure enough, the land was all that the Lord had promised. It was truly a land that "floweth with milk and honey." In fact, the grapes which they brought back were so robust that a cluster of them had to be borne on a staff supported on the shoulders of two men.

But the news was not all good. Ten of the returning spies reported that the people dwelt in very great walled cities: the Amalekites in the south; the Hittites, Jebusites, and Amorites in the mountains; and the Canaanites by the sea. But more than this, the giant sons of Anak dwelt there, before whom the spies felt as grasshoppers. In spite of the encouragement by Joshua and Caleb in the minority report, the people broke into open rebellion. God was leading them into the land but they were afraid and would not follow His leading.

The disobedience of Israel evoked the wrath of God. All Israelites twenty years of age and older were banned from ever dwelling in the land they had refused to enter. Instead, God declared they would wander in the wilderness for forty years, one year for each day the spies were in the land, and would die during that wandering. Only Joshua and Caleb were permitted to settle in the promised land for they alone were ready to move on God's command and according to His timetable.

When the people learned of God's sentence on their disobedience they were not at all penitent. Instead they resolved to atone for their sin by belatedly storming the promised land. But delayed obedience is the brother of disobedience. "And they *rose up early in the morning"* in preparation for their ill-fated campaign (Numbers 14:40). In spite of Moses' warning, the people marched against the Amalekites and Canaanites. What they would not do with God's help, they now attempted to do without it. First they refused to enter the land because of their unbelief in the power of God. Then they attempted to enter that same land because of their unbelief in the severity of God's judgment. In their own strength and outside of God's timing, they were sure to fail. They did. The enemy defeated the Israelites with a great slaughter and drove them back as far as Hormah.

Each of us who knows God must learn from Israel's tragedy so that it is not similarly repeated in our lives. We dare not question divine leading. If that leading is to dwell, as the Israelites did at the foot of Sinai, we must learn to be content where we are. But regardless of adverse circumstances, if God tells us that it is time to act, we have no reasonable choice but to act. Whether to remain indefinitely or move out immediately, we must learn to follow the accurate timetable of God. This can be done successfully only when we are sensitive to that still small voice of His Holy Spirit and are willing to obey it.

MORNING HYMN
> It may not be on the mountain's height,
> Or over the stormy sea;
> It may not be at the battle's front
> My Lord will have need of me;
> But if by a still, small voice He calls
> To paths I do not know,
> I'll answer, dear Lord, with my hand in Thine
> I'll go where you want me to go.

Good for Evil

MORNING SCRIPTURE   Genesis 26:17-35
MORNING VERSE   Genesis 26:31
And they rose up betimes in the morning, and sware one to another: and Isaac sent them away, and they departed from him in peace.

In his "Essay on Criticism" British author Alexander Pope inscribed the everlasting words, "To err is human; to forgive is divine." How easy it is to offend, yet how difficult to forgive the offense. The devil counsels you to hate your enemies, hinder them, and seek every opportunity to destroy them. Our Lord counsels, "Love your enemies, bless them that curse you, do good to them that hate you, and pray for them who despitefully use you, and persecute you" (Matthew 5:44). The words of the Lord Jesus sound very idealistic, but in the nitty-gritty of everyday life it is quite difficult to forgive someone who has purposefully persecuted you.

Consider the plight of Isaac. When a famine arose in Canaan, Isaac was driven south to dwell in the land of Gerar. Here Isaac sowed the land and the Lord blessed him one-hundredfold. The patriarch became a very great man with possessions of flocks and herds. This made the Philistines of Gerar envious and their king, Abimelech, asked Isaac to move elsewhere.

Thus Isaac departed in peace and pitched his tent farther south in the valley of Gerar. Immediately Isaac and his men redug the wells there which were previously owned by Abraham. Then Isaac's servants began to dig a new well. This brought strife with the herdsmen of Gerar who apparently did not want any more of the south country claimed by Isaac. The conflict was so great that Isaac named the well Esek, which means "contention." In order to avoid the problem, Isaac peaceably forsook that well and dug another. But this too brought the wrath of the Gerar herdsmen and Isaac named this well Sitnah (hatred). Again the well was given up in order to avoid confrontation. Isaac moved still farther south and his men dug yet a third well. This time they were apparently beyond the range of the envious herdsmen, for no strife followed. Isaac called this well Rehoboth meaning "wide space," where the Lord would make them fruitful in the land.

Shortly Isaac traveled north to Beersheba. When Abimelech learned that the increasingly wealthy and influential Isaac had come to Beersheba, he quickly paid him a visit. Abimelech hoped to regain the favor of Isaac whom he had earlier expelled. When Isaac inquired why Abimelech and his friends had come, they replied, "We saw certainly that the LORD was with thee: and we said, Let there be now an oath between us, even between us and thee, and let us make a covenant with thee; That thou wilt do us no harm, as we have not touched thee, and as we have done unto thee nothing but good, and have sent thee away in peace: thou art now the blessed of the LORD."

Abimelech and his friends were being quite gracious to themselves by saying that they had done Isaac nothing but good. In fact, they had uprooted him from fields which were giving a one-hundredfold yield. Even after he migrated south, the herdsmen of Gerar took possession of two of Isaac's tediously dug wells. Isaac had much to resent and be bitter about. But in typically godly fashion Isaac was willing to forgive the offenses against him.

A feast was made. Together they ate and drank. "And they *rose up betimes in the morning*, and sware one to another" (Genesis 26:31). Early the next morning they "cut a covenant," that is, they made a pact of peace that they would not harm one another. For Isaac this was a one-sided pact for he had wronged no one. He could have reacted angrily to the suggestion of the peace pact. But instead he forgave his offenders and dug another well at Beersheba (the "well of the covenant"). This confirmed the covenant with Abimelech.

To return evil for good is devilish; to return good for good is human; to return good for evil is godlike. The rich and powerful Isaac had no reason to forgive Abimelech and agree to the peace pact except that the love of God constrained him to do so. Isaac's forgiving spirit is reflected in our Lord's instruction, "Be ye, therefore, merciful, as your Father also is merciful. Judge not, and ye shall not be judged; condemn not, and ye shall not be condemned; forgive, and ye shall be forgiven" (Luke 6:36-37). It's good advice. Let's heed it today.

MORNING HYMN
> *More like the Master I would live and grow,*
> *More of His love to others I would show;*
> *More self-denial, like His in Galilee,*
> *More like the Master I long to ever be.*

Fruit and Faith

MORNING SCRIPTURE   Mark 11:1-26
MORNING VERSE   Mark 11:20
And in the morning as they passed by, they saw the fig tree dried up from the roots.

There is an old legend about a great teacher who was walking through an orchard on a windy day. The teacher came to a fence which divided the grove from an adjoining forest and he imagined that he could hear the trees talking to each other. The maple trees taunted a group of nearby fruit trees, "Why don't your leaves rustle in the breeze like ours so that you could be heard from a distance?" "We don't need such useless fluttering to draw attention to our presence," was the reply. "Our fruit speaks for us!"

The story of Jesus cursing the fig tree is a story of fruit and faith. As our Lord approached the cross during the Passion Week many outstanding events took place. On Palm Sunday He triumphantly entered the city of Jerusalem, but retired to the house of His friends in Bethany that evening. On the morrow He made His way back to the city of Jerusalem early in the morning. He was eager to be about His father's business and did not want to disappoint the people who would come early to hear Him teach in the Temple. Because He had risen early and left Bethany before the breakfast hour, Jesus and His disciples were hungry. On the way He spied a fig tree in full bloom.

The fig tree is unique in that the fruit appears on the tree before it comes to full bloom. Figs generally appear in February, followed by leaves later in the spring. Thus, when Jesus saw the tree in full bloom, He had every right to expect that there would be figs which He and the disciples could use for temporary sustenance. When He arrived at the tree, however, even though the tree was in full bloom, it was barren of fruit. Jesus cursed the tree saying, "No man eat fruit of thee hereafter for ever" (Mark 1 1:14).

When Jesus and the disciples returned *in the morning* to the site of the fig tree, they saw that the tree had dried up from its roots (Mark 11:20). The disciples were astonished at how rapidly the cursed tree had begun to disintegrate. When Peter called this phenomenon to the Master's attention Jesus said, "Have faith in God." The cursing of the fruitless fig tree was done deliberately to teach the lesson—"Have faith in God." Jesus continued to illustrate this when He said, "For verily I say unto you Whosoever shall say unto this mountain, Be thou removed, and be thou cast into the sea; and shall not doubt in his heart, but shall believe that those things which he saith shall come to pass he shall have whatsoever he saith" (Mark 11:23).

Some years ago a group of botanists went on an expedition to a remote part of the Alps. They were searching for new varieties of flowers. One day they saw a beautiful rare species growing at the extreme bottom of a deep ravine. It was almost impossible to get at. Someone would have to be lowered into the gorge to retrieve the rare flower. The botanist noticed a local Swiss boy standing nearby and asked him if he would get the flower. A rope would be tied around his waist and the men would lower him to the floor of the canyon. The young boy peered thoughtfully into the chasm. "Wait," he said, "I'll be right back." The lad dashed off. When he returned he was accompanied by an older man. The boy said to the scientists, "I'll go over the cliff now and get the flower for you but this man must hold the rope. He's my dad."

Fruit and faith go hand in hand. The incident of Jesus cursing the fig tree illustrates this beautifully. If we are to bear fruit we must have faith in the one who holds our hand. Whatever the task given to us, we will be only as successful in completing it as our faith in the Father will permit.

MORNING HYMN

> *I would be true, for there are those who trust me*
> *I would be pure, for there are those who care.*
> *I would be strong for there is much to suffer;*
> *I would be brave, for there is much to dare.*

Praising God

MORNING SCRIPTURE   Psalm 57:1-11
MORNING VERSE   Psalm 57:8
Awake up, my glory; awake, psaltery and harp: I myself will awake early.

The Psalms are the poetry of Palestine. They record the pains and pleasures, the distresses and delights of David and others. Over many psalms is a superscription, that is, an inscription which names the author of the psalm, sometimes gives the occasion for its writing, or the instrument upon which the tune is to be played. Although these superscriptions are not inspired of God as the individual psalms are, nonetheless they appear to be highly accurate and provide a good source of information for us regarding the psalms. The superscription for Psalm 57 says, "To the chief Musician, Altaschith, Michtam of David, when he fled from Saul in the cave."

King Saul had been openly seeking to take the life of David. Where could David turn for help? There was no question in his mind that the only place to turn for help was God. Thus he begins his psalm with the prayer, "Be merciful unto me, O God, be merciful unto me; for my soul trusteth in Thee. Yea, in the shadow of Thy wings will I make my refuge, until these calamities be overpassed." The psalmist knew that God would not permit the king to seek his life forever and that one day these calamities would be over. Although he would roam the hills of southern Palestine, nonetheless he would make his refuge the shadow of God's wings.

The first half of this psalm records David's cry to God for deliverance and salvation. He notes that there is someone "that would swallow me up" (Psalm 57:3) and that he lives "among lions...whose teeth are spears and arrows" (verse 4). David is fully aware that Saul has prepared a net for his steps and will relentlessly pursue him until the end.

Perhaps you too are being relentlessly pursued, not by the king but by financial distress or physical infirmities. What should your reaction be to these things? David's reaction, in

the midst of his distress and cry for help, was the positive statement of verse 5, "Be Thou exalted, O God, above the heavens;
let Thy glory be above all the earth." How could he say such a
thing, given his circumstances? How could he remain calm in
the midst of his storm? David provides the answer in verse 7,
"My heart is fixed, O God, my heart is fixed: I will sing and
give praise."

To sing praises unto God while we are being relentlessly
pursued by sickness, disease, and distress requires a heart that
is fixed on God and a tongue prepared to praise Him in the
midst of that pursuit. Thus the psalmist issues a threefold call
to awake himself to the praise of God. He says, "Awake up, my
glory." This is a call for his greatest intellect to give praise to the
Lord. The tongue can never express our praise to God until our
minds form that praise. Before we can praise God in the midst
of our troubles, we must have the mind to do so. David calls for
his glory, his intellect, to stir itself in praise of God.

Next he cries, "Awake, psaltery and harp." His fingers will
fly in joy over the strings of the psaltery and harp because his
mind has become fixed on God. He is determined to praise God
regardless of how his enemies pursue him. Let all the music
with which we are familiar be attuned to the praise of our God.

Finally he enjoins, "I myself *will awake early*" (Psalm 57:8).
No sleepy verses or weary notes will be heard from us early in
the morning. We will rouse ourselves to the highest calling of
man, to praise the Lord God among the people. We will faithfully, daily, arouse our intellect and will to the praise of God. We
will also employ our fingers and our tongues in praising Him
for His great deliverance. We will awake early to set ourselves
to that task, the noble task of praising God.

MORNING HYMN

> 'Tis the grandest theme thro' the ages rung;
> 'Tis the grandest theme for a mortal tongue
> 'Tis the grandest theme that the world e'er sung
> "Our God is able to deliver thee."

Walls of Water

MORNING SCRIPTURE   Exodus 14:1-31
MORNING VERSE   Exodus 14:24
And it came to pass, that in the morning watch the LORD looked unto the host of the Egyptians through the pillar of fire and of the cloud, and troubled the host of the Egyptians.

Everyone is aware of what can happen to the best laid plans of mice and men. But when the plans of men are in conflict with the purposes of God, they are destined for defeat. More than once the pages of Scripture record God's reversing an evil plan designed to destroy His people (cf. Esther 7:10; Daniel 3:22; 6:24).

The ancient Egyptians had been subjected to the ten most torturous plagues in history. The last of these plagues brought death to the firstborn of every Egyptian family, including the family of Pharaoh. The king called for Moses and Aaron and commanded them to get out of his land. Soon however, because his heart was bitterly hardened, Pharaoh regretted letting his Israelite slaves go, and quickly assembled the Egyptian armies, including an elite corps of six hundred chosen chariots. The troops mustered, Pharaoh pursued the Israelites and overtook them at Pi-hahiroth. God's chosen people were trapped. With the wilderness to Israel's side, the vast Red Sea before them, and the Egyptian armies closing in, a wretched grin must have crossed Pharaoh's face. There was no way out for Israel and the Egyptian king knew it.

Yet God had warned Moses not to fear but to stand still and see the salvation of the Lord. At nightfall, without warning, the angel of God removed the pillar of the cloud from before the Israelites and placed it between their camp and the Egyptian armies. From this vantage point the cloud lighted the breadth of the sea for the Israelites but, at the same time, obscured the view of the Egyptians, causing them to grope in the inky darkness. As Moses stretched forth his hand, the Lord caused an east wind to howl with such force that it pushed back the waters of the Red Sea. The children of Israel, six hundred thousand men plus women and children, crossed the sea on dry land between the walls of water. All night long the crossing proceeded. Finally the Egyptian charioteers apprehensively pursued God's people into the midst of the sea.

"In the morning watch the LORD looked unto the host of the Egyptians through the pillar of fire and of the cloud and troubled the host of the Egyptians" (Exodus 14:24). The Lord caused the wheels of the heavy Egyptian chariots to clog with mud and soon they began to break off. Panic-stricken and exhausted, they began to flee from the Israelites. But it was too late. The Lord commanded Moses to stretch forth his hand over the sea. When the first light of day appeared, the walls of water thundered together and not one Egyptian soldier was left. The bodies of Pharaoh's men washed ashore as a visible reminder to Israel of God's salvation.

Once a public school teacher, who was prejudiced against the Bible, was explaining to her class that the Jews' crossing the Red Sea was no miracle. "The water was only six inches deep," explained the godless teacher, "the Jews had nothing to worry about." From the back of the room came a little boy's shout "Praise the Lord, Hallelujah."

"No, Johnny, you didn't hear me correctly. I said the water was only six inches deep where the Jews crossed the Red Sea. It was no miracle."

Johnny replied, "Oh, that's not what I was praising the Lord for. I was praising Him for the miracle that Pharaoh's army could drown in just six inches of water."

Once again Israel's situation was completely reversed by God. That which was to be the downfall of the children of God proved to be their salvation. The Red Sea became a great symbol of victory instead of a story of defeat. Israel was now rejoicing in the Lord on the other side of a miracle.

MORNING HYMN
> *Safe is my refuge, sweet is my rest,*
> *Ill cannot harm me, nor foes e'er molest*
> *Jesus my spirit so tenderly calms,*
> *Holding me close in His mighty arms.*

Steps to Sin

MORNING SCRIPTURE   2 Samuel 11:1-27
MORNING VERSE   2 Samuel 11:14
And it came to pass in the morning, that David wrote a letter to Joab, and sent it by the hand of Uriah.

A historian once observed that Abraham Lincoln died in time to be great. That is, if he had lived longer, his greatness may well have been tarnished with mistakes. David was not so fortunate. He lived to make his greatest mistake and to commit his greatest sin with Bathsheba.

David was at war with the children of Ammon, east of the Jordan River. He sent Joab his captain to seize the city of Rabbah, what is today Amman, the capital of Jordan. David remained behind at Jerusalem perhaps because he had become self-indulgent and faced a growing inclination toward enjoying the luxurious life of the royal palace. At any rate, remaining behind ultimately led to his downfall. The steps which David took to fall into sin are characteristic steps. They are identical to those taken by Adam and Eve (Genesis 3), by Achan (Joshua 7:21), and by others. Here are those steps.

First, David was strolling in the evening on the roof of his palace when he saw a beautiful woman bathing in an adjacent house. Sin always begins with sight, or some sensual exposure. The sight of sin is not sin itself. Occasionally we cannot help but look upon sin. But the second glance at what we should not see is always sin.

Second, David "sent and inquired after the woman." Had he not given in to his lust for the bathing woman he would never have sent for information about her. In essence, he desired her and lusted after her when he knew he could not have her. The sight of sin the second time led David to illicit desire.

Third, 2 Samuel 11:4 indicates, "And David sent messengers, and took her." Like Eve in the garden of Eden and Achan at the battle of Jericho, David now actively participated in sin. These steps in the cycle of sin are universal; they cause us to stumble as well as David. We must be aware that one step always leads to the next, so that we can break this cycle. David failed to do so and it led to disgrace in the kingdom of Israel.

To have the king commit adultery was bad enough; but sin is never a private matter. It always involves others. Thus the *fourth* step in David's sin was to *involve* an innocent party in his sin. In this case the innocent party was Uriah the Hittite, the husband of Bathsheba.

When Bathsheba told David that she was with child and that it was his child, he unsuccessfully attempted to divert the consequences of his sin. He demanded that Uriah be returned to Jerusalem under the guise of wanting to know how the battle was going. He sent Uriah to his house, assuming that after Uriah had spent an evening at home with his wife everyone would assume that she was pregnant with his child. But Uriah would not enter the house. A disappointed David even attempted to get Uriah drunk so that he would go home, but to no avail. The die was cast; everyone would know that Bathsheba's child was not Uriah's.

In the morning David callously caused Uriah to be the bearer of his own death warrant to Joab (2 Samuel 11:14). As per the king's instructions, Joab placed Uriah in the heat of the battle so that he would be killed. David now added murder to the crime of adultery. This is hardly what we would expect from the man God had chosen to be king of Israel. It is what we have come to expect, however, when one lingers at the door of sin. Lingering at the door of sin is an open invitation to enter that door, and David stayed too long on the top of his roof while viewing the bathing Bathsheba. Had he fled from the presence of temptation he would not have entered the cycle of sin. You and I must flee temptation and the presence of evil if we would remain true to God. None of us has developed a resistant strain to the bacteria of sin.

MORNING HYMN
> Yield not to temptation, For yielding is sin
> Each vict'ry will help you Some other to win
> Fight manfully onward, Dark passions subdue,
> Look ever to Jesus, He will carry you through.

The Lord's Battle

MORNING SCRIPTURE   2 Chronicles 20:1-27
MORNING VERSE   2 Chronicles 20:20
And they rose early in the morning, and went forth into the
wilderness of Tekoa, and as they went forth, Jehoshaphat stood and
said, Hear me, O Judah, and ye inhabitants of Jerusalem; Believe in
the LORD your God, so shall ye be established; believe His prophets,
so shall ye prosper.

The battle of the forces of good against the forces of evil has raged on for millennia. Ever since Satan's heart was lifted up with pride and he said, "I will be like the most high" (Isaiah 14:13-14), the forces of God have been pitted against Satan and his forces in eternal conflict. This battle continues today with the apostle Paul reminding us that "we wrestle not against flesh and blood, but against principalities, against powers, against the rulers of darkness of this world, against spiritual wickedness in high places" (Ephesians 6:12).

One of the greatest difficulties in being a soldier in the army of the Lord is to recognize that we are but soldiers on the field of battle and not generals in the war room. We are called upon to fight Satan and his henchmen. We are engaged in hand-to-hand combat with the forces of immorality, ungodliness, and sin. Still, the battle is the Lord's, not ours. Nowhere is this truth more graphically illustrated than in the story of good King Jehoshaphat.

The quarter-century reign of Jehoshaphat, son of Asa, is one of the rare bright spots in Judah's checkered history. He was thirty-five years old when he ascended to the throne in 872 B.C. and continued the work of religious reformation and revival begun by his father. But, as is usually the case when a man attempts to serve God, the forces of Satan began to disrupt Judah during the days of Jehoshaphat. As 2 Chronicles 20:1 indicates, the peace of Judah was suddenly interrupted by a confederacy of the Moabites and Ammonites east of the Jordan River. The combined forces of this deadly duo were but a manifestation of the armies of Satan during that generation. What would the king of God's people do? Would he fight or would he knuckle under to Satan's stooges? Jehoshaphat did the only thing a godly person can do.

He "set himself to seek the Lord, and proclaimed a fast throughout all Judah."

When Jehoshaphat finished his prayer, Jahaziel, the son of Zechariah, who was in the line of Levites from Asaph, began to prophesy by the spirit of the Lord. He called to Judah and the inhabitants of Jerusalem and gave this message to the king and the people: "Thus saith the Lord unto you, be not afraid nor dismayed by reason of this great multitude; for the battle is not yours, but God's."

Reassured by this word from the Lord, the king and people bowed their faces to the ground and worshiped Jehovah the Lord. Then they stood to praise the Lord God of Israel with a loud voice. And, oh yes, they did one other thing: they put feet to their prayers. "*And they rose early in the morning* and went forth into the wilderness at Tekoa and as they went forth Jehoshaphat stood and said, hear me, O Judah, and ye inhabitants of Jerusalem; believe in the Lord your God, so shall ye be established; believe His prophets, so shall ye prosper" (2 Chronicles 20:20). Having prayed to God and armed with the knowledge that the battle was not theirs but His, the Jews arose early the next morning eager to be soldiers in God's army. When they arrived at the scene of battle they found no mighty armies, just dead bodies. Apparently the confused enemy fell on one another, Ammonites killing Moabites and Moabites killing Ammonites. Indeed, the battle was the Lord's.

This is a hard lesson to learn when the battle does not appear to be going God's way. Perhaps that's why so many soldiers today are discouraged and ready to desert the army of the Lord. But you and I must remember that we are taking our place in the Lord's army just as Jehoshaphat and the Jews took their places so many centuries ago. The battle still rages; the battle is still the Lord's. Let us pray to the Lord God for victory, praise His name for assurance, and then rush off early each morning to do battle with Satan and his armies throughout the day. We have the same confidence as did Jehoshaphat and the Jews, for we have the same God.

MORNING HYMN
Fierce may be the conflict, Strong may be the foe,
But the King's own army, None can overthrow;
Round His standard ranging, Vict'ry is secure,
For His truth unchanging Makes the triumph sure.
Joyfully enlisting, By Thy grace divine,
We are on the Lord's side—Saviour, we are Thine!

One God Alone

MORNING SCRIPTURE   1 Samuel 5:2-12
MORNING VERSE   1 Samuel 5:4
And when they arose early on the morrow morning, behold, Dagon was fallen upon his face to the ground before the ark of the LORD; and the head of Dagon and both the palms of his hands were cut off upon the threshold; only the stump of Dagon was left to him.

Periodically in history God chooses to reveal in dramatic fashion that He alone is God. When the shepherd boy David took on the mighty giant Goliath, he was confident of victory knowing that the Lord would deliver the giant into his hand, "That all the earth may know that there is a God in Israel" (1 Samuel 17:46). When Sennacherib, King of Assyria, threatened Jerusalem with invasion, and King Hezekiah was reminded that the gods of all the cities that fell before Jerusalem were unable to stay the Assyrian armies, Hezekiah fell before the Lord in prayer and said, "O LORD God of Israel, which dwellest between the cherubims, Thou art the God, even Thou alone, of all the kingdoms of the earth" (2 Kings 19:15). When Jehovah wills, He elevates Himself over all the false gods of the earth and proves that there is no God but Jehovah.

When Eli the priest was old and Samuel still young, God chose to show His superiority over the gods of the Philistines. With Israel encamped at Ebenezer and the Philistines at Aphek a mighty battle ensued. Israel was defeated and lost four thousand men in the fray. This completely devastated the Israelites for they remembered the mighty deeds which God had performed against their enemies in the past. Why was He not smiling on them now? Had Jehovah abandoned them? If so, how could they take Him into battle? They hit upon a plan.

"Let us fetch the ark of the covenant of the LORD out of Shiloh unto us, that when it cometh among us it may save us out of the hand of our enemies" (1 Samuel 4:3). They clung to the superstitious hope that the mere symbol of God's presence would be enough to bring them to victory. It wasn't. In the second battle thirty thousand men were slain, among them Hophni and

Phinehas, the licentious sons of Eli. But even worse, the ark of the covenant was seized by the hated enemy of Israel.

The Philistines took the ark of God and brought it to Ashdod, to the house of Dagon their god. Here the ark was placed before the idol. That night the Ashdodites slept with the sleep of sweet revenge.

Early on the morrow the Philistines arose to savor their victory (1 Samuel 5:3). But Jehovah God was up long before the Philistines arose and when they entered the temple of their god they saw Dagon fallen on his face before the ark of the Lord. It was the height of humiliation. It was as if Dagon had prostrated himself before the symbol of Jehovah. Quickly they returned the idol to its place and all the Ashdodites breathed a sigh of relief.

But once again Jehovah arose long before the Philistines for "when *they arose early on the morrow morning*, behold Dagon was fallen upon his face to the ground before the ark of the LORD" (1 Samuel 5:4). To add injury to insult, the head of the statue and both its hands were broken off so that only the stump of Dagon was left.

God allowed the ark to be captured by the Philistines to punish His superstitious people. But even in their punishment Jehovah was still jealous of His glory and when the Philistines should have been savoring their victory they were swallowing their pride.

Dagon was no match for Jehovah. The Philistines were learning what David had learned, what we all must learn. "Among the gods there is none like unto Thee, O LORD.... For Thou art great, and doest wondrous things: Thou art God alone" (Psalm 86:8,10). Since our God alone is God, let's praise Him today all the day long. We have a God who is a God of gods and worthy of our praise.

MORNING HYMN

> *A mighty fortress is our God,*
> *A bulwark never failing;*
> *Our helper He amid the flood*
> *Of mortal ills prevailing.*
> *For still our ancient foe*
> *Doth seek to work us woe*
> *His craft and pow'r are great,*
> *And armed with cruel hate,*
> *On earth is not his equal.*

Waiting on God

MORNING SCRIPTURE   Ezekiel 12:1-28
MORNING VERSE   Ezekiel 12:8
And in the morning came the word of the LORD unto me.

Have you ever watched a group of demonstrators carrying placards to call attention to their cause? Perhaps you have participated in a walk-a-thon to raise funds for a charity. Frequently people must do extraordinary things to gain publicity or call attention to their particular beliefs. There is a prophet in the Old Testament who did exactly the same thing at the direct command of God. His name was Ezekiel.

A contemporary of Jeremiah and Daniel, Ezekiel was a priest (Ezekiel 1:3), but never served as such because he was taken captive to Babylon during the reign of Jehoiachin (2 Kings 24:10-16). Ezekiel settled with a group of exiles at Tel-Abib, a town in the interior part of Babylonia on the river Chebar. Five years after he arrived in Babylonia, when he was about thirty years of age, Ezekiel received a call from Jehovah to prophesy to the people of the captivity.

Prophesying during the darkest days of the captivity, Ezekiel was met only with indifference and despondency among the people. The captive Jews would not listen to his message. Therefore God instructed Ezekiel to resort to a more dramatic method of proclaiming the destruction of Jerusalem. Instead of preaching or speaking in parables, he would act out the parable. Ezekiel would dramatize what God was about to do with His great city Jerusalem.

God reminded Ezekiel that he lived in a rebellious house amid a rebellious nation and that he should prepare to move out of that house. In order to be a visual representation of the captivity of Jerusalem, God commanded Ezekiel to "dig thou through the wall in their sight, and carry out thereby." So, packing his bags, Ezekiel proceeded to gouge out a hole in the mud wall of his house, making an opening onto the street through which he would pass with his baggage. There he would wait.

"And in the morning came the word of the LORD unto me"

(Ezekiel 12:8). Having waited all night, Ezekiel now gave an explanation to the Israelites for his rather unusual actions. Five times in this chapter the word of the Lord came unto Him; five times he had to wait on the word of the Lord. True, waiting in the comfort and privacy of his house would not have been as difficult as waiting on the sidewalk while everyone passed by, but waiting on God is never easy.

Sometimes the purposes and messages of God are revealed slowly. His grand designs can never be hurried. The great New England preacher Phillips Brooks was a man of great poise and quiet manner. Yet at times he suffered from moments of frustration when he had to wait on God. One day a friend saw him feverishly pacing the floor like a caged animal.

"What's the trouble, Mr. Brooks?" he asked.

"The trouble is that I am in a hurry, but God isn't!"

We can imagine that having clawed through the wall with bags in hand and waiting on the sidewalk for God to speak to him again was difficult for Ezekiel. Nonetheless, after God initially spoke to him, it was not until the morning that God came to him the second time. Ezekiel did as God commanded him without need for explanation. But then, in full view of everyone on the street, he must patiently wait on the Lord to speak to him again.

You and I must recognize that God leads us every step of the way, whether we understand His leading or not. To hear God say "Go" or to hear Him say "Stay" is usually easier than to hear Him say "Wait"! In potential ridicule, the prophet of God waited all night to hear the Lord God give him further instructions. How long are we willing to wait on God? Do we trust Him enough to wait on Him today?

MORNING HYMN

> *Not ours to know the reason why*
> *Unanswered is our prayer,*
> *But ours to trust God's wisdom still*
> *And to His love repair.*

Pleasing Worship

MORNING SCRIPTURE   Malachi 1:1-2:13
MORNING VERSE   Malachi 1:11
For from the rising of the sun even unto the going down of the same My name shall be great among the Gentiles; and in every place incense shall be offered unto My name, and a pure offering: for My name shall be great among the heathen, saith the LORD of hosts.

Although little or nothing is known of the personal life of Malachi the prophet, nonetheless he has given us one of the most interesting books in the Bible. Not only is this the last book of the Old Testament, it is also the last stern rebuke of the people of God, the last call for them to repent, and the last promise of future blessing for Israel.

In Malachi's day the people had become increasingly indifferent to spiritual matters. Religion had lost its glow and many of the people had become skeptical, even cynical. The priests were unscrupulous, corrupt, and immoral. The people refused to pay their tithes and offerings to the Lord and their worship degenerated into empty formalism. While the people had strong male lambs in their flocks, they were bringing blind and lame animals to be offered on the altars of Jehovah. Malachi was commissioned by God to lash out against the laxity of the people of God.

This prophecy is unique for it is a continuous discourse. In fact, Malachi has been called "the Hebrew Socrates" because he uses a style which later rhetoricians call dialectic. The whole of this prophecy is a dialogue between God and the people in which the faithfulness of God is seen in contrast to the unfaithfulness of God's people. Thus Malachi is argumentative in style and unusually bold in his attacks on the priesthood, which had become corrupt.

The most blistering attack in the entire book comes in Jehovah's dispute with His priests. If anyone should have known better than to fall to idolatry and corruption, it ought to have been those who served at the Temple of God. Still, the priests had again and again polluted the bread of the altar of God; they had sacrificed spotted animals on that altar and thus had made the table of the Lord contemptible. In addition to this, the priests were involved in empty formalism. They went about their duties day after day in dull drudgery rather than in faith. This was not pleasing to Him and Jehovah told them so.

In contrast, Jehovah declared the kind of worship that is acceptable: "For from *the rising of the sun* even to the going down of the same My name shall be great among the Gentiles" (Malachi 1:11). It is obvious this was not true in the days of Malachi, for the Gentiles had not yet come to praise the name of Jehovah. Nonetheless, Malachi is speaking prophetically and the day will come, the great millennial day, when all the nations of the earth will flock to the Temple in Jerusalem and there they will worship in sincerity the God of Israel. This worship will be carried on from the rising of the earliest sun to its setting hours later. All day long, service in that day will not be dull drudgery but will be a delightful duty.

What a contrast there is between the conclusion of the Old Testament and the conclusion of the New Testament. The Old Testament concludes with an invective against dead formalism in the church. The New Testament concludes with the bright and morning Star in the midst of the church. Thank God that prophecy does not end with the Old Testament but continues until the day that Jesus Christ will usher in an eternity with Him in Heaven. But let's not wait until then. Let's rise with the sun today and begin a day filled with praise to our God.

MORNING HYMN
> O worship the King, all glorious above,
> And gratefully sing His pow'r and His love;
> Our Shield and Defender, the Ancient of Days,
> Pavilioned in splendor and girded with praise.

Never Alone

MORNING SCRIPTURE   Genesis 28:1-22
MORNING VERSE   Genesis 28:18
And Jacob rose up early in the morning, and took the stone that he had put for his pillows, and set it up for a pillar, and poured oil upon the top of it.

The patriarch Jacob was a man rarely in solitude. His life was lived in rich association with others. The husband of four wives, Jacob fathered twelve sons of whom were descended the tribes of Israel. He could not even claim solitude at birth for he was the secondborn of twin sons. It seemed that Jacob's life was destined to be lived in association with others. Even when he died, Jacob was buried in the cave of Machpelah with his parents, grandparents, and wife Leah.

There was one occasion, however, when Jacob was alone, quite alone. After he had purchased the birthright from his brother Esau and had deviously received his father's blessing, Jacob set out to seek a wife. His father charged him not to marry a Canaanite but to journey to distant Paddan-aram and take a wife of the daughters of Laban, his mother's brother. This provided the perfect excuse for Jacob to flee from the wrath of his cheated brother, who had vowed to kill him.

Exiled from home and running from revenge, this solitary wanderer traveled north from Beersheba toward Haran. He camped on a remote plateau near the city of Luz. Here Jacob had time to ponder the events of his early life. Would the God of Abraham and Isaac be the God of Jacob as well? Was the covenant to extend to him? A sense of loneliness crept over him. Fear that his brother had followed him made Jacob apprehensive. He saw the figure of Esau behind every tree and rock. Finally, sheer exhaustion caused him to sleep, even with nothing but a stone for his pillow.

During the night Jacob had a dream. This was no ordinary dream, but a revelation from God. Jacob saw a ladder set up on the earth which reached into the heavens. Upon the ladder were the angels of God ascending and descending. But the most amazing feature of the dream was that at the top of the ladder stood the Lord Himself saying, "1 am the LORD God of Abraham...and, behold, I am with thee, and will keep thee in all places to which thou goest, and will bring thee again into this land, for I will not leave thee."

The words of God must have been music to Jacob's ears. The blessing which God had promised to Abraham and Isaac was now promised to Jacob as well. His lonely heart would never be lonely again. Jacob awakened with a start and gasped "Surely the LORD is in this place; and I knew it not.... And Jacob *rose up early in the morning,* and took the stone that he had put for his pillows, and set it up for a pillar, and poured oil upon the top of it," and called the place Bethel—the "house of God" (Genesis 28:18-19). Certainly this was a turning point in his religious life. When Jacob arose early that morning it was with a new attitude toward God. Jehovah was not some distant and unknowable god, but one who had been there, right in that very place. There was an open pathway of communication between God and men.

In essence, the revelation of this stairway to Jacob is a revelation of Jesus Christ. He is our ladder of communication to Heaven. With regard to salvation, Jesus Christ is our stairway through the stars to the God of Heaven. Jesus said, "I am the way, the truth, and the life: no man cometh unto the Father, but by Me" (John 14:6). But the Lord Jesus is so much more. To the Christian Jesus Christ is a continual, well-worn pathway to God. The Apostle Paul expressed it so clearly: "For there is one God, and one mediator between God and men, the man, Christ Jesus" (1 Timothy 2:5). The ladder of communication between God and men is Jesus Christ. He is our go-between, our mediator, our ladder of prayer.

Jacob was astounded to learn that communication between God and men was possible. Yet armed with that knowledge, he was no longer lonely. The Father's "I am with thee" to Jacob is God's promise to all His heirs. Jesus said, "And lo, I am with you alway" (Matthew 28:20). As the heir of God's promise we need never feel alone. We never are.

MORNING HYMN
> *When in affliction's valley I tread the road of care*
> *My Savior helps me to carry The cross so heavy to bear*
> *Tho' all around me is darkness, Earthly joys all flown;*
> *My Savior whispers His promise, Never to leave me alone!*

Wisdom and Riches

MORNING SCRIPTURE   Proverbs 8:1-36
MORNING VERSE   Proverbs 8:17
I love them that love me; and those that seek me early shall find me.

Proverbs belongs to that segment of the Old Testament designated as "wisdom literature." Such proverbial teaching represents one of the most ancient forms of instruction. The wisdom literature of Israel was the chief storehouse of moral and practical instruction for the Jews. It guided the head of state as well as the head of the home. It embodied the difference between right and wrong, righteousness and unrighteousness. But most of all, Israel's wisdom literature taught the Jews how to live before Jehovah. It contrasted the wisdom of the world, a wisdom of possessions, with the wisdom of God, a wisdom of piety.

Proverbs teaches us that all who would live godly must seek the wisdom of God and forsake the wisdom of the world. To seek divine wisdom, therefore, is to seek to know God better and to possess less. Wisdom is God and speaking as wisdom, God says, "I love them that love me; and those that *seek me early* shall find me" (Proverbs 8:17). God is to be sought early in life and early in each day of life. When we show Him we love Him in this way, He shows us He loves us by filling our day with His wisdom.

Seeking the wisdom of God and the God of wisdom does not necessarily mean we will be paupers on this earth. God says, "Riches and honor are with me; yea durable riches and righteousness. My fruit is better than gold, yea than fine gold; and my revenue than choice silver" (Proverbs 8:18-19). The revenue paid by seeking this world's wealth is temporal gain and a frequent deterrent to godliness. The revenue gained by seeking divine wisdom is eternal gain and an everlasting aid to godliness. Therefore, the truly wise person in this world will seek God's wisdom instead of the world's wealth. But should God allow us to have both, our attitude toward our possessions will be, "Every man to whom God hath given riches and wealth, and hath given him power to eat thereof, and to take his portion, and to rejoice in his labor; this is the gift of God" (Ecclesiastes 5:19).

An English nobleman once visited Josiah Wedgwood to see how he made his legendary china and pottery. A young apprentice was instructed to give the nobleman a tour of the factory. The nobleman didn't believe in God and was sacrilegious, foul-mouthed, and consistently ridiculed the Bible during the tour. At first the young apprentice was shocked but after awhile he began to laugh when the man made his cynical remarks. Josiah Wedgwood was greatly disturbed by this, especially when he saw how his young apprentice was being influenced by this wealthy nobleman. Later the atheist asked if he could purchase a particularly expensive vase. As he handed it to the nobleman, Wedgwood deliberately let it crash to the floor. With a vile oath the nobleman angrily said, "That's the one I really wanted and now it's shattered by your carelessness." Josiah Wedgwood replied, "Sir, there are things more precious than any vase—things that can never be restored once they are ruined. I can make another vase, but you can never give back to my helper the pure heart you've defiled by your vile language and sacrilegious talk!"

The nobleman was an example of a man who did not seek the Lord early but sought riches all the day. Josiah Wedgwood is a fine example of a man who early sought the Lord and recognized that his wealth was a gift from God. God never intended that we should not have riches; He only intended that riches should not have us. It is vitally important for Christians who possess wealth not to be possessed by it. Seek the wisdom of the Lord early in the day before earning the wealth of the world. Then use that wealth in a way which will bring eternal reward.

MORNING HYMN
I take, O cross, thy shadow For my abiding place
I ask no other sunshine than The sunshine of His face
Content to let the world go by, To know no gain nor loss,
My sinful self my only shame, My glory all the cross.

Obeying God

MORNING SCRIPTURE   Acts 5:12-32
MORNING VERSE   Acts 5:21
And when they heard that, they entered into the temple early in the morning, and taught.

There is a legend in Greek mythology about an old sailor who was piloting his ship through the rough waters of a stormy sea. In his extremity, he stood erect and cried to the gods, "Father Neptune, you may sink me if you will, or you may save me if you will, but whatever happens, I will keep my rudder true!" While sailing the tempestuous Aegean Sea, this old captain exhibited the kind of determination necessary for anyone who would stand by his convictions.

In the development of the early Church, the apostles and early followers of the Lord Jesus frequently found themselves at odds with the Roman government and with the Jewish religious establishment. Acts 5 records that the high priest rose in indignation, accompanied by the Sadducees, and cast the apostles into the common prison for preaching in the name of Jesus of Nazareth. But while they were incarcerated, an angel of the Lord appeared, opened the prison doors during the night, and set the apostles free. The command of the Lord's angel was, "Go, stand and speak in the temple to the people all the words of this life." With renewed freedom and determination the apostles "entered into the temple *early in the morning* and taught" (Acts 5:21). Although they knew that teaching in the name of the Lord Jesus would most certainly mean additional imprisonment, these apostles obeyed the word of the Lord rather than the wishes of man.

When it came to the attention of the religious officials that these apostles were again teaching in the Temple, the indignation of the Jews rose to a fever pitch. The captain of the Temple and the chief priests once again brought them before the council and the high priest asked, "Did not we straitly command you that ye should not teach in this name? And, behold ye have filled Jerusalem with your doctrine, and intend to bring this man's blood upon us." Now the situation worsened; the apostles were faced with the decision whether to defy the direct orders of the religious senate and avoid persecution or to accept the persecution as a consequence of standing up for their beliefs. As usual, Peter was the spokesman and said, "We ought to obey God rather than man." The die was cast. Unashamed of the gospel of Christ, these apostles chose certain imprisonment rather than disobey the direct command of God to preach in the name of Jesus.

Frederick the Great once invited some notable people to his royal table, including his top-ranking generals. One of them was Hans von Zieten, a devout Christian. Von Zieten declined the emperor's invitation because he wanted to attend a communion service at his church. At a subsequent banquet Frederick the Great and his guests mocked the general for his religious beliefs and derided the Lord's Table. In great peril of his life, the officer stood to his feet and said respectfully to the monarch, "My lord, there is a greater king than you, a king to whom I have sworn allegiance even unto death. I am a Christian and I cannot sit quietly as the Lord's name is dishonored, His character belittled, and His cause subjected to ridicule. With your permission I shall withdraw." The other generals present at this occasion trembled in silence, knowing that von Zieten might well be killed for his stand. But to their surprise, Frederick grasped von Zieten's hand, asked his forgiveness, and requested that he remain. Frederick promised that he would never again make light of such serious spiritual matters.

Occasions do arise when we must obey God rather than men. When they arise, we must be willing to suffer the consequences, whether it be ridicule, as in the case of Hans von Zieten, or even imprisonment, as in the case of the apostles. That to which we are subjected because of our stand for Christ is not our concern. Our concern is that we take the stand.

MORNING HYMN

> *Stand up, stand up for Jesus,*
> *The trumpet call obey;*
> *Forth to the mighty conflict*
> *In this His glorious day.*
> *Ye that are men now serve Him*
> *Against unnumbered foes;*
> *Let courage rise with danger*
> *And strength to strength oppose.*

Reaction or Response

MORNING SCRIPTURE   Mark 15:1-20
MORNING VERSE   Mark 15:1
And straightway in the morning the chief priests held a consultation with the elders and scribes and the whole council, and bound Jesus, and carried Him away, and delivered Him to Pilate.

A converted Hindu woman had suffered much at the hands of her unsaved relatives. One day a missionary asked her, "When your husband is angry and persecutes you, what do you do?" The Hindu woman replied, "I just cook the food better and sweep the floor a little cleaner. When he speaks unkindly, I answer him mildly, trying to show him in every way that when I became a Christian I also became a better wife." Although that husband had resisted all the efforts of the missionaries, he could not resist the sweet silence of his Christian wife. The Holy Spirit used her to win him to Christ.

How do you react when you meet antagonism? When you are mistreated or wrongly accused, do you harbor resentment or seek revenge? Do you attempt to retaliate or verbally abuse those who have abused you?

Jesus had been led away to the high priest. His agony in the garden had been interrupted by His betrayal. To make matters worse, His primary disciple, the Apostle Peter, had denied Him three times. Our Lord had endured both physical and verbal abuse all night long. *"And straightway in the morning* the chief priests held a consultation with the elders and scribes and the whole council, and bound Jesus, and carried Him away, and delivered Him to Pilate" (Mark 15:1). As the Sanhedrin gathered early on the morning of Jesus' crucifixion, they attempted to make the trial official, yet their single purpose was "to put Him to death" (Matthew 27:1).

Jesus was falsely arraigned, falsely accused, and falsely abused. Yet to all of the trumped-up charges, to all of this pseudoevidence, our Lord made no reply. When the chief priests continued to accuse Him falsely of many things, Mark records that the Lord Jesus answered nothing. So uncharacteristic was it for a person falsely accused not to rise to His own defense that Pilate asked astonishingly, "Answerest Thou nothing?" But the narrative repeats, "Jesus yet answered nothing." It was nothing short of remarkable that Jesus would not retaliate or lash out against those who had treated Him so cruelly and unjustly.

A young sergeant was serving the British army in Egypt under the Highland Regiment. This solider was an effervescent and shining Christian. When he was asked how he came to know the Lord Jesus as Saviour, he recounted his conversion by saying, "There is a private in this company who was converted in Malta before the regiment came to Egypt. We gave that fellow an awful time. On one terrible night he came in very tired and wet. But before getting into bed, he knelt down to pray. My boots were soaked with water and covered with mud, and I let him have it with one on the side of his head, and struck him with the second on the other side. But he just went on praying. The next morning I found those boots beautifully polished and standing by the side of my bed. That was his reply to me, and it just broke my heart. I was saved that day."

Our response to those who lie against us must never be to lash out against them. As we arise early in the morning, perhaps after a day in which our character has been slandered and our conduct has been slashed, we must arise with a commitment to live a life like the Lord Jesus who, when He was reviled, reviled not again. Only then will we live happily in a world filled with unhappy people.

MORNING HYMN
> *Bearing shame and scoffing rude,*
> *In my place condemned He stood—*
> *Sealed my pardon with His blood:*
> *Hallelujah, what a Saviour!*

Personally Known

MORNING SCRIPTURE   Psalm 88:2 -18
MORNING VERSE   Psalm 88:13
But unto Thee have I cried, O LORD; and in the morning shall my prayer prevent Thee.

We have today as our Scripture the darkest, most mournful psalm in the Psalter. This psalm is unique in that it is the only psalm in which the outpouring to God of a burdened heart fails to bring relief or consolation.

Yet, as terrible as the despair of the psalmist is, he is not in utter despair. No one who utterly despairs will pray, for prayer is the proof of lingering hope. Even in the midst of despair, the psalmist recognizes that, should there be any hope, it will be found only in God (Psalm 88:1-2,9,13).

Have you ever felt alone? Have you ever felt abandoned, even by God? Have you ever felt you have been left to face the world and its trials all by yourself? If so, you can join the rest of us and the writer of this psalm. He felt he had been abandoned by God, that he was all alone. The psalmist was concerned that he was not getting through to God, that his prayers were not being heard. God appeared to be unmoved by his prayers.

With a trouble-filled soul, the psalmist was convinced that his "life draweth nigh unto the grave" and that he was numbered "with them that go down into the pit." He had been afflicted with waves of the wrath of God. Night and day he wept because of his affliction. He says, "But unto Thee have I cried, O LORD; and *in the morning* shall my prayer prevent Thee" (Psalm 88:13). Day after day he arose before the dawn and began to pray before the sun was up. He was consistent in seeking the face of the Lord early in the morning. Still no resolution was given to his problem. No answer came from God.

Perhaps the psalmist felt God did not know who he was. Perhaps he was just another face in the crowd, unknown to the Lord of Heaven. Perhaps he was just too insignificant for God to take time to hear his prayer. All of these were a "perhaps" in his mind. None of them was true.

There is a small arctic sea bird called the guillemot that lives on the rocky cliffs of northern coastal regions. These birds flock together by the thousands in comparatively small areas. Because of the extremely crowded conditions, the females must lay their pear-shaped eggs side by side in a long row on a narrow ledge. All the eggs look alike, yet the mother bird knows exactly which one is hers. If someone disturbs the eggs and moves one of them, the mother guillemot is able to find her egg among the thousands and return it to its original location. To the human eye the eggs appear as if they have been mass produced on an assembly line. To the guillemot, each egg is known personally, identified personally, and attended personally.

The Bible is clear that our heavenly Father is even more intimately acquainted with His own children than the mother guillemot is with her egg. He knows us, He knows us personally. He even knows the number of hairs on our heads. He can tell identical twins apart. He knows every thought and emotion we have, and He understands all the decisions we make. He gives personal attention to each of us in all our affairs from morning until night.

So great is our Lord's loving concern for our lives that Jesus told His disciples the Father knows when a single sparrow falls upon the ground. Since human beings are of much greater value than the fowls of the air, we can certainly be assured that He knows all about us. We are the object of His constant care and attention. We have not been abandoned by God, nor as His child will we ever be abandoned.

MORNING HYMN
> *Be not dismayed whate'er betide,*
> *God will take care of you;*
> *Beneath His wings of love abide,*
> *God will take care of you.*

God's Provision

MORNING SCRIPTURE   Exodus 16:1-21
MORNING VERSE   Exodus 16:7
And in the morning, then ye shall see the glory of the LORD; for that He heareth your murmurings against the LORD: and what are we, that ye murmur against us?

I f we enjoyed the vantage point of Heaven, above both space and time, we would readily see the hand of God guiding us through history. The continuity of God's dealings with mankind would then become quite evident for we would not be bound by the years of one lifetime. But because we cannot rise above space and time does not mean we are left without insight into God's providential leading through history. Using types and symbols, the Bible miraculously illustrates the essential unity between the Old and New Testaments. By comparing the prophetic types of the Old Testament with their fulfillment in the New, we see that history is proceeding on the course designed by God before time began.

One month after the children of Israel walked away from Egyptian bondage and crossed the Red Sea, they struck a course inward from the sea to the Wilderness of Sin. Their unleavened bread was exhausted and they began to face the hunger and thirst of the sandy desert. The Israelites murmured that they had it better back in Egypt and should have remained there. But the Lord promised Moses He would rain bread from Heaven to feed the starving Israelite multitudes. Moses relayed the message. *"And in the morning,* then ye shall see the glory of the LORD; for that He heareth your murmurings against the LORD"(Exodus 16:7). This heavenly bread, referred to as manna, was like the coriander seed of the parsley family but resembled the silver white hoarfrost which covered the ground on Middle Eastern mornings. It tasted like wafers made with honey.

This manna is a type of Christ, foreshadowing God's provision for mankind centuries later. Our Lord said, "Verily, verily, I say unto you, He that believeth on Me hath everlasting life. I am the bread of life. Your fathers did eat manna in the wilderness, and are dead. This is the bread which cometh down from heaven, that a man may eat thereof, and not die. I am the living bread which came down from heaven; if any man eat of this bread, he shall live forever; and the bread that I will give is My flesh, which I will give for the life of the world" (John 6:47-51).

The similarities between the Old Testament type, the manna, and the New Testament fulfillment, Jesus Christ, are striking. The pure white manna descended noiselessly in the night without fanfare. The Christ child was born on a silent night without fanfare. The heavenly manna was to be gathered early each morning. Nine verses of this chapter refer to the morning. Not only are we to seek the Lord Jesus early in the day (Psalm 63:1), but early in life as well (Ecclesiastes 12:1).

The manna was clearly a gift from God. Israel did not earn this bread; in fact, this murmuring lot didn't even deserve it. God's salvation is never earned or deserved. "For by grace are ye saved through faith; and that not of yourselves, it is the gift of God" (Ephesians 2:8). Manna was God's gift of life to the Israelites. Jesus Christ is God's gift of life to all mankind. Without God's gift of manna, the undeserving Israelites would have died. But without God's gift of Jesus Christ, the bread of life, all the world would be condemned to death.

God's hand is guiding history today as it always has. The theme of His life-giving provision spans the ages. This is the message of God which runs through the centuries: "For God so loved the world, that He gave His only begotten Son, that whosoever believeth in Him should not perish, but have everlasting life" (John 3:16). Past, present, or future, God's provision is always there for those who will receive it.

MORNING HYMN
> *Guide me, O Thou great Jehovah,*
> *Pilgrim thro' this barren land*
> *I am weak, but Thou art mighty,*
> *Hold me with Thy pow'rful hand.*

Commitment

MORNING SCRIPTURE   Hosea 6:1-11
MORNING VERSE   Hosea 6:4
O Ephraim, what shall I do unto thee? O Judah, what shall I do unto thee? for your goodness is as a morning cloud, and as the early dew it goeth away.

C ommitment: an absolute dedication and faithfulness to someone or something. It's something we all claim to have, yet very few demonstrate. Many people claim to have a strong commitment to the local church, yet rarely attend even when they have nothing else to do. Others take wedding vows which include promises of commitment, yet those vows are broken rapidly and all commitment is nullified. Nothing is so distressing to the Lord God as to see a Christian who is only half committed to Him (see Revelation 3:14-22).

The greatest example of a lack of commitment in the Old Testament is found in the prophecy of Hosea. Hosea (whose name means "salvation") was a prophet to the northern kingdom and a contemporary of Amos. In fact, Hosea was to the northern kingdom what Jeremiah was to the southern kingdom—a weeping prophet. His prophecy is very tender and his ministry similar to that of John the Apostle.

The purpose of Hosea's prophecy was to provide Israel with a real-life example of her spiritual idolatry. Hosea transferred his personal tragedy into a figure of the tragedy of Israel as a nation. The lack of commitment to him by his wife and her infidelity was but a minute calamity when compared with the spiritual infidelity of Israel and their lack of commitment to God. Hosea called Israel to national repentance much as he pleaded with his adulterous wife for personal repentance.

To bring Israel to understand how complacent they had become, the prophet observed, "Your goodness is as *a morning cloud,* and as the early dew it goeth away" (Hosea 6:4). Israel's commitment was shallow at best and Hosea likened the fleeting goodness of uncommitted men to a morning cloud and the early dew which vanishes with the morning sun. God is never pleased with such a halfhearted commitment and a complacent attitude toward Him. Israel had not yet learned that lesson; apparently twentieth century Christians haven't either.

There is a tiny harbor town on the ocean shore where many ships have crashed on the rocks in violent weather. This town became well-known because of the dedicated rescue team which aided mariners in distress. The rescue team would rally to the sound of the siren and rush to the scene of the accident, risking life and limb to save the sailors from drowning. As time went on, the citizens of that tiny town raised enough money to build a rescue station close to the shore. While this greatly facilitated the operation, it softened the dedicated team as well. As time went by they added some of the comforts and conveniences that other rescue stations had. Through the years the rescue station became a social club where the town's people gathered to have fun and relax. Ships would still crash upon the rocks, the alarm would still sound, but eventually no one responded. They were reluctant to leave their comforts because their commitment to rescue the miserable mariners was no match for their complacency.

We can imagine that Hosea felt much the same way about Israel as we may feel toward this once dedicated rescue team. Still, there are many Christians today who have a halfhearted attitude toward God and, in fact, have committed spiritual adultery with the world just like Hosea's wife. Much of Christianity today is nothing more than "country club Christianity," basking in the goodness of God, relying on the riches of this world's goods, and unconcerned about commitment to the Father or about the rescue of those who are perishing.

We can almost hear Hosea saying, "Your goodness is as *a morning cloud*, and as the early dew it goeth away." The fleeting goodness of uncommitted Christians is not goodness at all. It is just a temporary rest stop on the highway to complacency.

MORNING HYMN

A charge to keep I have—
A God to glorify,
Who gave His Son my soul to save
And fit it for the sky.

Haunting Sin

MORNING SCRIPTURE   2 Samuel 15:1-18
MORNING VERSE   2 Samuel 15:2
*And Absalom rose up early, and stood beside the way of the gate:
and it was so, that when any man that had a controversy came to
the king for judgment, then Absalom called unto him, and said, Of
what city art thou? And he said, Thy servant is one of the tribes of
Israel.*

Sin has an uncanny way of coming back to haunt us. After
David committed the double crimes of adultery and murder with Bathsheba and Uriah, the Lord sent the prophet
Nathan unto him with a parable designed to convict David of
his sin. When Nathan said to David, "Thou art the man" (2
Samuel 12:7), David immediately realized the grievousness of
his error. He said, "I have sinned against the LORD" (2 Samuel
12:13). Although God forgave that sin, David still had to bear the
consequences of it. The child that was produced as the result of
the king's lust died, and others of David's children became ruth-
less and rebellious, plotting against his life.

Punishment for David was swift in coming. Before his marriage to Bathsheba, David had sixteen sons who lived as princes
among the people, each one in his own house. Only three of them
are of any note in history: the eldest, Amnon, son of Ahinoam of
Jezreel; the third, Absalom, son of Maacah of Geshur; and the
fourth, Adonijah, son of Haggith. Both Absalom and Adonijah
plotted against their father and sought to overthrow him.
Amnon's sin was equally despicable.

Absalom had a sister named Tamar who was exceptionally
beautiful. Amnon became so enamored of her that he fell sick.
Marriage with a half sister was forbidden by the Mosaic law and
thus Amnon opted for an alternative course of action. By force
he seduced Tamar and caused her to lie with him. Subsequently
he hated her and fled from the scene. When Absalom arrived
and queried Tamar about Amnon, the truth was known. So enraged was Absalom that he immediately began to plan for revenge against Amnon.

After two years of seething, Absalom invited the king with

all his sons, Amnon in particular, to a sheep-shearing feast at Baal-hazor, on the border of Ephraim. Amid the festivities Absalom's servants slew Amnon when he was merry with wine. As a result, Absalom fled from David to the house of his grandfather, Talmai, King of Geshur, and there remained three years until David sent to retrieve him

Immediately upon returning from his exile, Absalom began to undermine the authority of his father. As 2 Samuel 15:2 says, "And Absalom *rose up early,* and stood beside the way of the gate." Absalom wanted to get an early start to meet all who came to Jerusalem for a judgment about any controversy. When he questioned the parties involved he couched his language in a way that made him look good and his father look bad. Then he would suggest, in his best political style, "Oh that I were made judge in the land, that every man which hath any suit or cause might come unto me, and I would do him justice!" Sin usually appears in a smooth-talking package and Absalom, already a handsome man, was sweet-talking the affections of the Israelites away from David their king, the man anointed of God. By conversation dripping with false honey, a handshake, and an insincere kiss to strangers, Absalom "stole the hearts of the men of Israel."

So successful were Absalom's traitorous schemes in winning the hearts of the Israelites that he was soon able to go to Hebron, announce himself as king, and rally to his side the majority of the Israelite nation. But Absalom was not the man of God's choosing to succeed David as king, and God would have no part of it.

While David was learning that sin has a way of haunting one, Israel was about to learn a valuable lesson too. It is not always the man with the sweetest smile, the warmest handshake, or the honey-dipped words who has our best interests at heart. Such wolves in sheep's clothing would never gain a foothold in our hearts if we were given to consistent consultation with God about those who would be leaders over us. Let's pray for our leaders today and for those whom God would have lead us tomorrow.

MORNING HYMN
All the way my Saviour leads me; What have I to ask beside?
Can I doubt His tender mercy, Who thro' life has been my Guide?
Heav'nly peace, divinest comfort, Here by faith in Him to dwell
For I know, whate'er befall me, Jesus doeth all things well.

Upward Eyes

MORNING SCRIPTURE   2 Kings 6:8-23
MORNING VERSE   2 Kings 6:15
And when the servant of the man of God was risen early, and gone forth, behold, an host compassed the city both with horses and chariots. And his servant said unto him, Alas, my master! how shall we do?

Once a British newspaper carried a story about two famous men, one an artist and the other a novelist. It read: "James McNeill Whistler and Oscar Wilde were seen yesterday at Brighton talking, as usual, about themselves." Whistler clipped the notice and sent it to his friend with this comment: "I wish these reporters would be more accurate. If you remember, Oscar, we were talking about me." Wilde responded with a telegram saying, "It is true, Jimmie, we were talking about you, but I was thinking about myself." Although this incident may be amusing, it does show a dreadful quality in human nature. We are so self-centered and have our eyes so firmly fixed upon ourselves that we do not see others around us or God's activity in our behalf.

Israel had been harassed by many incursions from Damascus throughout their history, and the king of Syria was once again issuing mandates in a tone which the king of Israel could not accept. During these predatory incursions from Syria, King Jehoram of Israel was saved again and again through warnings of danger by the prophet Elisha. As a result, the Syrian king believed a traitor was in his midst warning Jehoram and thus allowing the Israelite king to escape from the snares laid for him. But such was not the case; the courtier advised the king of Syria there was no informant, simply the man of God who "telleth the king of Israel the words that thou speakest in thy bedchamber."

This enraged Ben-hadad to such an extent that he sent his Syrian armies to Dothan, where Elisha was dwelling, to capture the prophet and prevent future lifesaving revelations to the king of Israel. The Syrian armies with their horses and chariots and a great host came by night and encompassed the city.

When Elisha's servant *was risen early* and went for a morning stroll, he spied the massive armies with horses and chariots (2 Kings 6:15). Immediately he became terrified and ran to Elisha gasping, "Alas, my master! how shall we do?" Elisha's response to the rattled servant was a classic example of calm in the midst of the storm. He said, "Fear not; for they that be with us are more than they that be with them."

Although the armies encamped against Elisha and his servant were formidable, nonetheless Elisha knew that his servant would not be so fearful if only he could get his eyes off himself and his enemies and see the host of Heaven that God provided to protect him. Thus Elisha prayed that Jehovah would open the eyes of his servant and when the Lord responded the young man saw that "the mountain was full of horses and chariots of fire round about Elisha." Then the servant knew the angel of Jehovah encircles those that fear God and delivers them. He had taken his eyes off himself and gazed on God's unlimited resources to protect them.

Soon the armies of Syria attacked and once again Elisha prayed, "Smite this people, I pray thee, with blindness." This Jehovah did and in the confusion Elisha persuaded the enemies' armies to follow him to the man they came to slay. Little did they know that the same man was about to lead them to Samaria, Israel's capital city, where the prophet again prayed, "Lord, open the eyes of these men that they may see." The astonished Syrian soldiers discovered that they were in the very midst of Samaria. God had delivered Israel's enemies into their hands in a miraculous way.

If we get our eyes off problems and on their solution, off our circumstances and on the God who controls them, off ourselves and on Him, there's no telling what God will do for us.

MORNING HYMN

> 'Tis so sweet to trust in Jesus
> Just to take Him at His Word,
> Just to rest upon His promise;
> Just to know, "Thus saith the Lord."
> Jesus, Jesus, how I trust Him!
> How I've proved Him o'er and o'er!
> Jesus, Jesus, precious Jesus!
> O for grace to trust Him more!

Revival

MORNING SCRIPTURE   Nehemiah 8:1-18
MORNING VERSE   Nehemiah 8:3
And he read therein before the street that was before the water gate from the morning until midday, before the men and the women, and those that could understand; and the ears of all the people were attentive unto the book of the law.

In the months that followed the rebuilding of Jerusalem's wall, Ezra and Nehemiah worked together to improve the social and religious conditions of the people. They were greatly aided by the prophet Malachi. The end result of the fine work of these three preachers was the greatest revival meeting in history. Described in chapter 8, this revival meeting can be characterized as follows.

1. The greatest revival meeting in attendance (verse 1). "And all the people gathered themselves together as one man into the street that was before the water gate." No Jew was excluded from this meeting. They were not sent engraved invitations; they were there out of the joy of the Lord.

2. The greatest revival meeting in length (verse 3). At this meeting Ezra the scribe brought the book of the Law of Moses, "And he read therein, before the street that was before the water gate *from the morning* until midday" (verse 3). Having assembled themselves early, the people never flinched when Ezra stood up to read and read from dawn's early light until the hot rays of the afternoon Palestinian sun.

3. The greatest revival meeting in array of preachers (verse 4). As Ezra stood behind the pulpit of wood, he had on the platform with him thirteen other preachers, presumably all to take their turn at preaching and reading the Scriptures.

4. The greatest revival meeting in attention from the congregation (verse 5). When Ezra opened the book, "all the people stood up." Evidently the people, as well as the preachers, stood from early in the morning until midday. Their deep reverence for God's Word would not permit their attention to be diverted.

5. The greatest revival meeting in revival spirit (verse 6). When Ezra and the others finished reading the Word of God,

they blessed the Lord, the great God. To this "all the people answered, Amen, Amen, with lifting up their hands; and they bowed their heads, and worshiped the LORD with their faces to the ground."

6. The greatest revival meeting in results (verses 7-8). Verse 8 summarizes this great revival with the words, "So they read in the book in the law of God distinctly, and gave the sense and caused them to understand the reading." Hearing the Word of God and understanding it brought the people to a spontaneous outpouring of tears. Personal revival is frequently accompanied by such tears.

7. The greatest revival meeting in celebration (verses 10-12). When Nehemiah, Ezra, and the Levites saw the tremendous effect that the reading of the Word had on the people, they commanded them to get up, go to their homes, eat, and rejoice in the Lord. This was a holy day and having expressed remorse for their sins, they could now enter into the week-long celebration of the Feast of the Tabernacles, fully aware of Jehovah's forgiveness for their sins.

Years ago evangelist Gypsy Smith was conducting meetings when a preacher came and asked the secret of his success. He wanted to know what the best method would be for starting a spiritual awakening in his own congregation. Gypsy Smith's answer, "Brother, go home and lock yourself in your room. Take a piece of chalk and draw a circle on the floor. Then get down on your knees inside that circle and confess all your known sins. Determine to follow the Lord wherever His Word directs you, no matter what the cost. Ask Him to begin His work in you! When this prayer is answered, you will have the beginning of a revival in your church."

If we want to see a revival in our country similar to that of Jerusalem in Nehemiah's day, perhaps we should lock ourselves in our rooms with a piece of chalk. Let's pray for a revival in our own hearts today.

MORNING HYMN
> *We praise Thee, O God! For the Son of Thy love,*
> *For Jesus who died, And is now gone above*
> *Hallelujah! Thine the glory; Hallelujah! Amen!*
> *Hallelujah! Thine the glory; Revive us again.*

God's Perfect Will

MORNING SCRIPTURE   1 Samuel 9:15—10:1
MORNING VERSE   1 Samuel 9:26
And they arose early: and it came to pass about the spring of the day, that Samuel called Saul to the top of the house, saying, Up, that I may send thee away. And Saul arose, and they went out both of them, he and Samuel, abroad.

Samuel had been a judge for many years and was yielding to advanced age. Who would lead the people after his death? Like the sons of Eli before him, both of Samuel's sons, Joel and Abiah, had disqualified themselves for they had "turned aside after lucre, and took bribes, and perverted judgment" (1 Samuel 8:3). If Israel did not choose a king and Samuel died, anarchy would once again prevail as it had in the days of the judges, when everyone did "that which was right in his own eyes" (Judges 17:6).

Besides, without a king Israel was missing out on all the pomp and ceremony that the other royal courts of the ancient Near East enjoyed. While the Jews were wandering nomads, unsettled and without a homeland, they cared little about what other nations did or had. But now they had become firmly established in the promised land and all the surrounding nations had a king. Why not Israel?

In the permissive will of God, Saul was to be that king. The son of Kish, a wealthy and influential Benjamite, Saul as choice for king may appear to the untrained eye as a matter of pure chance. Sent by his father to round up some stray donkeys and failing to locate them, Saul decided to appeal to Samuel the prophet for assistance in locating the strays. The day before God had forewarned Samuel that on the morrow a Benjamite, whom he should anoint to be captain over Israel would approach him. When Saul arrived there was little question in the priest's mind about his identity. Blessed with natural graces and talents, not to mention that he was head and shoulders taller than any of the other Jews, Saul was the natural selection for king of Israel. But more than this, in the permissive will of God, his was also the supernatural selection. Jehovah had decided to give Israel her wish, for better or for worse, and Saul was His selection for the man who would be king.

As the Benjamite approached Samuel the word of Jehovah came to the priest and he said, "Behold the man." Led to the banquet chamber of the high place, Saul and his servant were seated above the thirty guests who had assembled there. Samuel instructed the cook to bring the best portion of the meat from the sacrifice and place it before Saul. More than this, something that is rarely done, Samuel invited Saul to stay with him that night and sleep upon the top of the house. *They arose early* after communing through the night and made their way through the city where Samuel took a vial of oil, poured it upon Saul's head, gave him the kiss of homage, and anointed him as captain over the Lord's inheritance, the nation Israel (1 Samuel 9:26).

To live in God's permissive will is but to receive temporary blessing. Saul is one of the great tragic figures of Old Testament history. Although selected by God at the cries of the people, he degenerated into a psychopathic condition in which his powers were sapped and his kingdom was rent from his hands. Rejection, defeat, and suicide were the inevitable results.

Perhaps a mere coincidence, it is nonetheless striking that when the priest encountered the man who in God's permissive will would become king of the Jews he said, "Behold the man" (1 Samuel 9:17). Centuries later when Pilate encountered the man who in God's perfect will would become King of the Jews, he likewise said, "Behold the man!" (John 19:5). Saul's reign was immediately accepted by the people because he was handsome and they anticipated he would lead Israel successfully into battle against her enemies. Jesus' reign was immediately rejected by the people for He had "no form nor comeliness" and He never intended to lead His people victoriously against Israel's enemy. Saul was Israel's choice; Jesus is God's choice. How much better off we are to live in His perfect will rather than to settle for His permissive will.

MORNING HYMN

> *Simply trusting ev'ry day,*
> *Trusting through a stormy way;*
> *Even when my faith is small,*
> *Trusting Jesus that is all.*

Partnership

MORNING SCRIPTURE   Genesis 31:17-55
MORNING VERSE   Genesis 31:55
And early in the morning Laban rose up, and kissed his sons and his daughters, and blessed them: and Laban departed, and returned unto his place.

T he Lord watch between me and thee, when we are absent one from another" (Genesis 31:49). How frequently these words are used as a benediction, especially at the close of a church service. They seem to express the prayer of two parties for mutual protection by the Lord until such time as they are safely and happily reunited. However, the context in which these words were uttered compels just the opposite conclusion.

Jacob was a scoundrel. He took advantage of his twin brother Esau by persuading him to sell the birthright for a mess of pottage. Later Jacob lied to his father and tricked Isaac into bestowing on him the irrevocable family blessing. Even Jacob's name means "supplanter, one who removes or replaces by scheming or treachery." Yet he met his match in father-in-law Laban. When Jacob reached Haran he spied the beautiful Rachel and agreed to serve Laban seven years for her hand in marriage. At the end of those seven long years Laban tricked Jacob by switching his daughter Leah for Rachel. This meant another seven years of labor for the girl Jacob loved. In all, the patriarch served fourteen years for Laban's daughters and six years for a herd of cattle.

At the end of this time God reminded Jacob of the vow he made to return to the promised land. Jacob asked Laban to release him and permit his return to Bethel. This, however, would have ruined Laban financially. Scoundrel that he was, Jacob was still heir to the promise of God and Laban knew that the secret of his own increasing wealth was God's blessing on Jacob. Therefore Laban proposed that Jacob forget about leaving and become his partner. This meant that Jacob's only recourse was to depart secretly from Haran while Laban was away shearing his sheep.

Aware that she would receive no inheritance from her father, Rachel removed the family gods as she prepared to leave Laban's house. Archaeological excavations at Nuzi in northern

Mesopotamia indicate that when the household gods (teraphim) were in the possession of a son-in-law, he was legally designated as the principal heir. For this reason Rachel stole her father's gods without the consent or knowledge of Jacob.

When Laban learned of his son-in-law's hasty departure he pursued Jacob and his family. Seven days later at Mount Gilead Laban overtook them and immediately confronted Jacob about the stolen gods. Having no knowledge of them, Jacob permitted a search to be made. The gods, cleverly hidden by Rachel, were not found and this only served to increase the distrust between father and son-in-law. It was obvious that the suspicion between the two could not continue indefinitely. Therefore a covenant was devised which would not permit either party to further impede the other. Sworn to at Mizpah, the terms of the covenant were simple. A pile of stones was erected as a heap of witness between Laban and Jacob that from that day forward neither one would pass beyond that heap in order to do the other harm. Since the only witness to this event was God, the two men said, "The LORD watch between me and thee, when we are absent one from another." Suspicion and distrust are clearly present in this malediction. *"Early in the morning* Laban rose up, and kissed his sons and his daughters, and blessed them,"* returning to Haran (Genesis 31:55). He is never heard from again in the narrative of Scripture.

Jacob, the man of God, had made a covenant with Laban, the man of the world. The Bible does not prohibit God's children from making necessary pacts with the world. Frequently such business covenants or contracts are made. However, the Bible does warn against making unequal partnerships or yokes with the world (2 Corinthians 6:14). For twenty years Jacob carefully eluded making such a yoke with Laban even though he was his father-in-law. The man of God knew that a lifetime with the world, enticing and profitable as it may have seemed, was no substitute for the blessings of the promised land. Christians today still need to learn that lesson.

MORNING HYMN

> *I am resolved no longer to linger,*
> *Charmed by the world's delight;*
> *Things that are higher, things that are nobler,*
> *These have allured my sight.*

Reformation

MORNING SCRIPTURE   2 Chronicles 29:20–30:12
MORNING VERSE   2 Chronicles 29:20
Then Hezekiah, the king, rose early, and gathered the rulers of the city, and went up to the house of the LORD.

U nlike the ten northern tribes of Israel which had only downs, the two tribes of Judah to the south had their ups and downs. Just five or six years before the northern kingdom came to an end with the fall of Samaria, Hezekiah became king of Judah. As the thirteenth king of Judah, Hezekiah succeeded his father Ahaz in the third year of Hoshea, the nineteenth and last king of Israel. He was twenty-five years old when he began to reign and had a long reign of twenty-nine years in Jerusalem.

In contrast to his father, Hezekiah proved to be the most faithful to Jehovah of any of Judah's kings since David. It is said of him, "And he did that which was right in the sight of the LORD, according to all that David his father had done" (2 Chronicles 29:2). Ben Sira, the ancient historian, reckons Hezekiah with David and Josiah as the only three kings who did not forsake the law of the Most High God. Of him it is written, "He trusted in the LORD God of Israel; so that after him was none like him among all the kings of Judah, nor any that were before him. For he clave to the LORD and departed not from following Him, but kept His commandments which the LORD commanded Moses. And the LORD was with him; and he prospered whithersoever he went forth" (2 Kings 18:5-7).

In the very first month of his reign, Hezekiah set in motion the most thorough religious revival that Judah had ever known. This revival began by reopening and repairing the doors of the Temple which had been closed by Ahaz, and by cleansing and purifying that sacred edifice. Undoubtedly the prophet Isaiah had a beneficial influence on Hezekiah to initiate such a revival. There is even a Jewish tradition that he was a cousin of King Hezekiah. Regardless, he is said to have prophesied in the reign of four kings of Judah: Uzziah, Jotham, Ahaz, Hezekiah

117

(Isaiah 1:1). Together, Isaiah as prophet and Hezekiah as king, they would restore the religion of Israel to the worship of Jehovah.

In just eight days the house of the Lord was restored and sanctified. The report came back to Hezekiah that the priests and Levites had cleansed the house and the altar of burnt offerings with all the vessels and the table of shewbread thereof. These had been discarded during the reign of Ahaz.

After all had been made ready, "Hezekiah the king *rose early*, and gathered the rulers of the city, and went up to the house of the LORD" (2 Chronicles 29:20). The priests made the appropriate sacrifices and the Levites with cymbals, psalteries, and harps began to praise the Lord with music. All the congregation worshiped, the singers sang, and the trumpeters blew their trumpets. It was a joyous occasion indeed. All that were present with the king bowed themselves with Hezekiah and worshiped Jehovah. And this was only phase one of Hezekiah's great revival.

In phase two he sent word to all Israel and Judah that they should come to the house of the Lord at Jerusalem and keep the Passover. This is the first recorded ceremony of Passover-keeping since the time of Joshua, hundreds of years earlier. How low the people of God must have sunk during these turbulent years.

The heart of Jehovah must have been thrilled to see a man so concerned with the spiritual well-being of His people that he would restore the house of God, cleanse it, reinstitute the services and sacrifices in it, and rise early in the morning to worship Him. All of this was just the beginning of Hezekiah's reforms. How it would thrill the heart of Jehovah to see a man like Hezekiah raised up today to reform the worship of Israel once again. Let's pray to that end. Pray for the salvation of God's people and for the peace of Jerusalem.

MORNING HYMN
> *Revive Thy work O Lord!*
> *Thy mighty arm make bare;*
> *Speak with the voice that wakes the dead,*
> *And make Thy people hear.*

God's Unfailing Word

MORNING SCRIPTURE   Luke 21:1-38
MORNING VERSE   Luke 21:38
And all the people came early in the morning to Him in the temple, for to hear Him.

T hroughout His teaching ministry Jesus enjoyed an increasing appreciation for His message. Thousands thronged around Him, not only to view His powers of healing and raising the dead, but also to hear His words. Jesus was more than a prophet, a priest, and a king. The gospel writers describe Him as a preacher and a teacher as well. Just before the Passion Week Luke records that Jesus taught daily in the Temple, "And all the people came *early in the morning* to Him in the temple, for to hear Him" (Luke 21:38). His message was not just novel; it was truth.

Much of what Jesus taught daily in the Temple was prophetic in nature. In the early part of Luke 21 Jesus passed through the temple treasury and commented on the splendor of the magnificent Temple. However, Jesus predicted that it would be destroyed and His words are descriptive of the days leading up to the destruction of Jerusalem by the Romans in A.D. 70.

The latter half of this chapter is a prophecy concerning Jerusalem during the great tribulation period of this earth. He describes it as a time in which there shall be signs in the sun, the moon, and the stars. Men's hearts will fail them for fear. The powers of the heavens shall be shaken. Jesus taught the crowds who followed Him early in the morning to the Temple that God would unleash His vengeance on a sinful world before the Son of Man rode out of Heaven in power and great glory to establish His kingdom on this earth (cf. Revelation 19:11-16).

As the people came daily to hear the teachings of the Lord He knew that His time was quickly coming to an end on this earth. Therefore He reminded them that "Heaven and earth shall pass away: but My words shall not pass away" (Luke 21:33). It is evident that the Word of God, whether given verbally by the

Lord Jesus or inscribed by God in the Holy Bible, is more un-shakable than the universe itself. The same God who has the power to shake the very heavens also has the power to make unshakable His Word. While the heavens will not stand according to the prophecy of Jesus, the Word of God will always stand.

Today, in the twentieth century, Jesus does not speak to us and teach us as He did early in the morning in the Temple, but He still speaks to us through His Word, God's Word—the Holy Bible. We have the benefit of hearing the very same teaching that these heard who came at the dawning of the day to the Temple. We can sit at the feet of Jesus today by reading His Word.

H. A. Ironside told of a godly man named Andrew Frazer who had come to southern California to recover from a serious illness. Though this Irishman was quite weak, he opened his worn Bible and began expounding the truths of God's Word in a way that Ironside had never heard before. So moved by Frazer's words was Ironside that his curiosity drove him to ask, "Where did you learn these things? Did you learn them in some college or seminary?" The sickly man said, "My dear young man, I learned these things on my knees on the mud floor of a little sod cottage in the north of Ireland. There with my open Bible before me I used to kneel for hours at a time and ask the Spirit of God to reveal Christ to my soul and to open the Word to my heart. He taught me more on my knees on that mud floor than I ever could have learned in all the seminaries or colleges in the world."

To spend time in the Word of God yields a much richer understanding of the deep things of theology than to spend time in a classroom. For the person denied a formal education in Bible and theology, there is no shame if we spend time at the feet of Jesus. From early in the morning, throughout the day, and into the evening hours the great scholars of the Word become so because of time spent in God's book and on their knees Each of us has the same opportunity to do that. Let's take that opportunity today.

MORNING HYMN
Thy Word is like a garden, Lord, With flowers bright and fair;
And ev'ryone who seeks may pluck A lovely cluster there.
Thy Word is like a deep, deep mine, And jewels rich and rare
Are hidden in its mighty depths For ev'ry searcher there.

Effective Prayer

MORNING SCRIPTURE   2 Kings 19:1-37
MORNING VERSE   2 Kings 19:35
And it came to pass that night, that the angel of the LORD went out, and smote in the camp of the Assyrians an hundred fourscore and five thousand. and when they arose early in the morning behold, they were all dead corpses.

K ing Hezekiah was in a jam. Although he had trusted God, and did that which was right in the sight of the Lord, nonetheless his Assyrian enemy was knocking at his door. Sennacherib had sent three of his lieutenants to Jerusalem with a great host of Assyrian soldiers. Rab-shakeh, the spokesman for this terrible trio, taunted the Israelites, ridiculing their faith in Jehovah. He stood before the wall of Jerusalem shouting obscenities to the Jews and counseling them, "Let not Hezekiah deceive you...Neither let Hezekiah make you trust in the LORD...hearken not to Hezekiah.... Make an agreement with me" (2 Kings 18:29-31).

When the king heard that the Assyrians were outside the city walls, he rent his clothes, covered himself with sackcloth, and went into the house of the Lord. Here Isaiah the prophet encouraged Hezekiah that God had the situation well in control. Soon Hezekiah received a letter from the king of Assyria demanding that he surrender the city. What Hezekiah did next is characteristic of a man of faith. Hezekiah prayed unto the Lord God and in his prayer we can see the elements of all righteous prayer

1. His prayer was *instinctively spontaneous* (verse 14). When Hezekiah received the threatening letter, he immediately spread it before the Lord. There was no thought of calling a committee or seeking the advice of others; Hezekiah knew what to do, as did Elisha (2 Kings 4:33) and Nehemiah (Nehemiah 2:4) in similar situations.

2. His prayer was *praisefully reverent* (verse 15). He addressed Jehovah as, "O LORD God of Israel which dwellest between the cherubims, Thou art the God, even Thou alone." The Lord's Prayer (Matthew 6:9) indicates the same kind of reverence.

3. His prayer was *intimately personal* (verse 16). After he addressed God in a reverent fashion, Hezekiah said, "LORD, bow down Thine ear and hear" He had recognized God as sovereign; now he addresses Him as friend.

4. His prayer was *respectfully informative* (verses 17-18). Hezekiah did not demand of God what should be done. He was reminding himself in prayer of what God had promised. When we inform God of our situation in prayer, it is not because He is unaware of how desperate we are; we do it so we are aware of how desperate we are.

5. His prayer was *purposefully direct* (verse 19a). The time had come to get down to business. He pointedly made his request known unto the Lord. "O LORD our God, I beseech thee, save Thou us out of his hand." Hezekiah did not mince words; he was direct and forthright in his request to God.

6. His prayer was *properly motivated* (verse 19b). Hezekiah prayed for deliverance from the Assyrians, "that all the kingdoms of the earth may know that thou art the LORD God, even Thou only." Anything that happens to God's people reflects on God's purpose. Our prayers ought to be motivated so that the world sees the grace of God in our deliverance from desperate situations.

7. His prayer was *powerfully effective* and 2 Kings 19:35-36 shows the powerful effect of the righteous man's prayer "And it came to pass that night, that the angel of the LORD went out, and smote in the camp of the Assyrians an hundred fourscore and five thousand: and when they arose *early in the morning*, behold, they were all dead corpses." Early the next morning Hezekiah and the Jews found their enemy routed and 185,000 dead soldiers. God had performed what He promised.

Prayer is the power that gets ahold of God. Each of us would be wise to study carefully Hezekiah's prayer and see how these seven characteristics of his prayer can be applied to our prayer lives. Let's be like Hezekiah and believe that "the effectual fervent prayer of a righteous man availeth much" (James 5:16).

MORNING HYMN
> *I must tell Jesus all of my trials,*
> *I cannot bear these burdens alone;*
> *In my distress He kindly will help me,*
> *He ever loves and cares for His own.*

Our Majestic God

MORNING SCRIPTURE   Exodus 19:1-25
MORNING VERSE   Exodus 19:16
And it came to pass on the third day in the morning that there were thunders and lightnings, and a thick cloud upon the mount, and the voice of the trumpet exceeding loud; so that all the people that was in the camp trembled.

The waning years of the twentieth century will undoubtedly be remembered both as an era of mushrooming technology and vanishing virtue. As the world's scientific achievements increase, its moral discernment declines. Institutions once sacred are now scorned. Beliefs that our less sophisticated forefathers revered and respected are now relinquished and ridiculed. The last third of this century has spawned a noticeable decrease in reverence and this tendency is nowhere more evident than in religion. Even the church has a grossly inadequate appreciation of who God is and how He should be revered.

In the third month after the exodus, Israel entered the desert of Sinai and encamped at the foot of the great mountain. As God's representative, Moses was summoned to Mount Sinai. Here God revealed that He would make Israel a "peculiar treasure" unto Himself above all other people. They would be a kingdom of priests and a holy nation if they would but obey God's voice and keep His covenant. Moses returned to the people with this proposition and they all agreed.

In three days the covenant would be established but the holiness of Almighty God is so awesome that much preparation would have to be made before the Israelites could enjoy His presence. Only the pure in heart can "see" God. Moses was to sanctify the people for two days. They were to wash their clothes, an outward sign of the fact that they were inwardly clean. This cleansing within must stem from a heartfelt repentance, deep contrition, and a sincere desire to live righteously before God. Such preparation each man had to make for himself. In addition, fences or barriers were to be set up in public preparation to meet God. To impress Israel with the awesome majesty of God and the reverence with which they should meet Him, the mountain was itself declared holy—off limits to everyone but Moses and Aaron. None could touch it or even approach it beyond the fences.

With the preparations made and the people standing by in silent awe, "It came to pass on the third day *in the morning*, that there were thunders and lightnings, and a thick cloud upon the mount, and the voice of the trumpet exceeding loud; so that all the people that was in the camp trembled" (Exodus 19:16). The reverence for God that this event was designed to instill in Israel renders vain any attempt to describe adequately the scene.

The Holy One of Israel appeared in a thick cloud because His presence was awesome, too tremendous to be seen physically. Accompanying the clapping of thunder was the voice of the trumpet, exceedingly loud. So terrifying was the trumpet that the people in the camp below were dumbfounded. They stood in mute reverence to the holiness of Almighty God. The whole mountain quaked greatly, shaking from top to bottom, as the people stood in amazement.

The awfulness and terror of this event is even more remarkable when we consider that God was not descending to Mount Sinai as Israel's Judge. He was not about to pronounce a sentence of doom on them but in love He was drawing them unto Himself through the Sinai covenant. The smoke, fire, cloud, trumpet, lightning, and thunder were all to bring Israel to revere Him for He is holy and almighty. He is of incredible majesty

Although it is the duty of the Christian to praise God, it is our first duty to revere and fear Him. He alone is worthy of all reverence. "Wherefore receiving a kingdom which cannot be moved, let us have grace, by which we may serve God acceptably with reverence and godly fear; For our God is a consuming fire" (Hebrews 12:28-29). Let's revere the Lord today, and spend some time praising Him for who He is.

MORNING HYMN

> *Praise ye the Lord, the Almighty,*
> *The King of creation!*
> *O my soul praise Him,*
> *For He is thy health and salvation!*
> *All ye who hear,*
> *Now to His temple draw near;*
> *Join me in glad adoration!*

Morning Mercies

MORNING SCRIPTURE   Lamentations 3:1-36
MORNING VERSE   Lamentations 3:22-23
It is of the LORD's mercies that we are not consumed, because His compassions fail not. They are new every morning, great is Thy faithfulness.

The book of Lamentations may be the saddest writing in the ancient Near East. Composed of five chapters, each chapter is an elegy, almost a funeral dirge. Each of these elegies is sad beyond description. The whole of the book of Lamentations is a poem of pain, a symphony of sorrow. Lamentations has been called the wailing wall of the Bible, and so it is. The tears shed with each distressing chapter only increase as the Lamentations progress. There is but one bright spot in the five lamentations. This bright spot is our devotional for today.

In the midst of the most monstrous dirge of despair, the Prophet Jeremiah issues a remarkable testimony to the breadth and the force of divine grace. The black clouds which characterize the Lamentations are not universal; there is a minute break in those clouds through which the brightest sunlight streams forth. The penetrating rays of Lamentations 3:22-23 find their way through the chinks and crannies of the deepest dungeon. In the midst of his despondency over the destruction of Jerusalem, Jeremiah sees a ray of hope which depicts the unceasing mercies of God.

Although we have no claim on God's mercies, and they are altogether undeserved, nonetheless they never cease. We have done much to provoke God and give Him cause to cut off His mercy in our behalf. We have abused His mercy, ignored His mercy, even at times ungratefully accepted His mercy. Still, while God's mercies may not always be visible, they are always present. The mercies of God may change their form, as the morning light varies from the evening light, but the mercies of God will never cease to give their light. Even chastisement is mercy in disguise and frequently, under the circumstances which make chastisement necessary, it proves to be more merciful than had not God chastised us at all.

In the ray of sunlight presented by Lamentations 3:22-23, we learn that not only are the mercies of God not consumed, "They are new *every morning*" proving the great faithfulness of God.

There is great novelty in human life. Each day brings to us new and difficult problems, new and exciting challenges. God's mercy is ever-present with us, but the form it takes is ever-changing. God adapts His mercy to our immediate needs of each day. His mercies are not chiseled in stone but are vital and vibrant. We need not exhume the antique mercies which God showered on Moses, Jeremiah, or John. God's mercies on our behalf are fresh and alive today As God renews His world by greening it every spring, so too He refreshes and invigorates His people by renewing His mercies to them every morning.

With every new morning, nature offers a tribute of praise to God's mercy The sun rises, the birds sing, the trees sway in the breeze. Shall we alone be silent and ungrateful? Shall the Christian, who has the most reason to praise God for His mercy, be slow to acknowledge that God's mercy is renewed to him each day? Will we allow the natural creation of God alone to praise its Creator?

No matter how dark our day may appear to be, let us remember this with Jeremiah, "It is of the LORD's mercies that we are not consumed, because His compassions fail not. They are new every morning, great is Thy faithfulness" (Lamentations 3:22-23).

MORNING HYMN
>Great is Thy faithfulness, O God my Father!
>There is no shadow of turning with Thee;
>Thou changest not, Thy compassions, they fail not:
>As Thou hast been Thou forever wilt be.
>Great is Thy faithfulness! Great is Thy faithfulness!
>Morning by morning new mercies I see;
>All I have needed Thy hand hath provided—
>Great is Thy faithfulness, Lord, unto me!

A Long Day

MORNING SCRIPTURE   Acts 28:1-31
MORNING VERSE   Acts 28:23
*And when they had appointed him a day, there came many to him
into his lodging to whom he expounded and testified the kingdom
of God, persuading them concerning Jesus, both out of the law of
Moses, and out of the prophets, from morning till evening.*

Bible students find many parallels between what they read in the Word of God and what they see in the animal kingdom. Many of God's creatures have been singled out as examples of various kinds of activities. We are all familiar with the expression, "Busy as a bee." Although perhaps not as noticeable, the activity of others of God's creatures is just as great as that of the bee. For example, the thrush gets up at 2:30 every morning, begins work at once and does not stop until 9:30 at night. That's a whole nineteen-hour day. During that period of time this bird feeds its hungry fledglings about two hundred times. While the busyness of the bee is more noticeable, the activity of the thrush is equally as productive.

Astounding parallels can be drawn between the life of the Apostle Paul and the busy activity of the bees and the long days of the thrush. When Paul was saved on the road to Damascus, the Bible says, "Straightway he preached Christ in the synagogues, that He is the Son of God" (Acts 9:20). Paul may have said something like this to God at his salvation, "Lord, if you save me, the world will never hear the end of it!" It never did.

In this last chapter of Acts the apostle completes his tortuous journey to Rome and arrives to be placed under house arrest until his hearing before Caesar. It would have been a time for rest, recuperation from the rigors of the voyage, and restoration. No one would have criticized Paul for a lack of activity. He could have rationalized that to preach Christ in this situation only would have jeopardized his case before Caesar and perhaps ultimately cut short his ministry. Still, "There came many to him into his lodgings; to whom he expounded and testified the kingdom of God, persuading them concerning Jesus both out of the law of Moses and out of the prophets, *from morning till evening*" (Acts 28:23).

He had just spent two years in prison at Caesarea. Since he was a Roman citizen, his final appeal was always to Caesar. While enroute to Rome a tempestuous wind arose, the ship was tossed to and fro for fourteen days and finally ran aground. With the others, Paul had to swim to shore, clinging to broken pieces of the ship. As if that were not enough, on shore he was bitten by a viper, but did not die. After three months they continued their journey, finally arriving at Rome. All this occurred just before Acts 28:23. From early in the morning until late at night he continued his preaching and teaching activity No one asked him to put in such a long day, especially after the trials of the preceding months. Paul did it as a volunteer in the service of the Lord.

More importantly, the busyness of his activity was not in defense of his apostleship or in spinning yarns of his shipwreck. His activity was entirely a witness to the grace of God. He expounded and testified of the kingdom of God and persuaded them of the messiahship of Jesus. He had the right method; he preached unto them. He had the right message; he preached Jesus unto them. He had the right manner; he preached Jesus unto them from morning until evening.

Even toward the end of his recorded ministry, the Apostle Paul put in a long day of activity for the Lord. You and I have the same responsibility, the same opportunity, the same message as did the apostle. We must be as busy as a bee and put in a day like the thrush, with the message which stirred the heart of the apostle, if we are to rest at the end of this day fully satisfied of our service to the Lord God. Let's make sure we're satisfied tonight.

MORNING HYMN

> *Give of your best to the Master,*
> *Give Him first place in your heart;*
> *Give Him first place in your service,*
> *Consecrate ev'ry part.*

God's Abiding Presence

MORNING SCRIPTURE 1 Samuel 11:1-15
MORNING VERSE 1 Samuel 11:11
And it was so on the morrow, that Saul put the people in three companies; and they came into the midst of the host in the morning watch, and slew the Ammonites until the heat of the day: and it came to pass, that they which remained were scattered, so that two of them were not left together.

O nce in scorn an unbeliever asked a Christian, "Where is God?" The Christian immediately responded, "Let me first ask you, 'Where is He not?'"

Saul had become Israel's first king but his leadership had not yet been tested. He did not have to wait long, however, until an opportunity arose for him to lead Israel decisively. During the latter years of Samuel's life the enemies of Israel had gained significant strength. One of those enemies was the Ammonites who dwelt east of the Jordan River. Nahash, the Ammonite, marched against the city of Jabesh-gilead, which was nestled in the thickly wooded hills east of the Sea of Galilee. This fertile farm district was of great importance to the Ammonites who generally lived in an arid land.

When Nahash laid siege to Jabesh-gilead he offered the inhabitants of the city an opportunity to make a covenant with him and to serve him as docile slaves. This probably would have been accepted had not Nahash made one unacceptable provision in this covenant. In utter contempt, he would only accept servitude from the Israelites if they would agree to allow him to put out the right eye of all the inhabitants of the city. In an unusual act of mercy, the Ammonites permitted the Israelites seven days to make their decision.

Immediately a Gileadite runner was dispatched to bring this distressing news to Israel's new king. Nahash's audacity fanned the spark of leadership in Saul and he immediately took a yoke of oxen and hewed them in pieces, sending one piece to each tribe throughout Israel and warning them that they would meet a similar fate if they did not rally behind Samuel and himself to fight against the Ammonites. Immediately three hundred thousand warriors of Israel and thirty thousand men of Judah assembled at Bezek in order to march on Gilead and repel the Ammonite forces.

A message was sent ahead to the men of Jabesh-gilead saying that tomorrow, by the time the sun was hot, they would have help from the rest of Israel. *On the morrow* Saul moved into the host of the Ammonites *in the morning watch* with three army divisions and slew them until the heat of the day (1 Samuel 11:11). The victory over Ammon was complete. God acted swiftly and early in the morning.

Perhaps Nahash the Ammonite attempted to enslave the city of Jabesh-gilead because it was on the eastern side of the Jordan River. Maybe he thought that the God of Israel resided only in the promised land and would not be concerned with the two and one-half tribes in the hinterland. But God's people have His promise that He is always close at hand. "Do not I fill heaven and earth saith the LORD?" (Jeremiah 23:24). God's abiding presence is ever with His people and Satan and his henchmen must never feel free to lay siege to the people of God just because they are living on the fringe of God's activity.

A nineteenth century Scottish churchman named Chalmers once wrote, "When I walk by the wayside, He is along with me, when I enter into company amid all my forgetfulness of Him, He never forgets me. In the silent watches of the night, when my eyelids are closed and my spirit has sunk into unconsciousness, the observant eye of Him who never slumbers is upon me. I cannot flee from His presence. Go where I will, He leads me, and watches me, and cares for me."

If you are one of God's children, you need never feel forsaken, abandoned, or alone. You need never worry about the attacks of men like Nahash simply because you dwell where there is lessened opportunity for service to the Lord or in years when bustling activity for the Lord has passed you by. God is as much interested in the two and one-half tribes of Israel east of the Jordan as He is in the tribes dwelling in the promised land. You have the promise of His abiding presence just as much as others do. Claim that promise throughout this day.

MORNING HYMN
Anywhere with Jesus I am not alone;
Other friends may fail me, He is still my own;
Tho' His hand may lead me over dreary ways,
Anywhere with Jesus is a house of praise.

Yielding to God

MORNING SCRIPTURE   Genesis 32:1-32
MORNING VERSE   Genesis 32.24
And Jacob was left alone; and there wrestled a man with him until the breaking of the day.

J acob was in big trouble. He was caught between his two greatest enemies. Behind him was his avaricious father-in-law, Laban. Before him was his vindictive brother, Esau. The patriarch wasn't exactly on speaking terms with either of these men. He had secretly left Laban's household in order to return to the promised land. Would Laban now honor the covenant they had made at Mizpah (Genesis 31:49)? Jacob wasn't sure. But even if Jacob had nothing to fear from Laban, there was still Esau.

Earlier in his life Jacob had craftily deprived his twin brother of both his birthright and his father's blessing. Now for the first time in twenty years he was about to encounter the brother whom he had wronged. Esau had become a powerful man in Mount Seir, the land of Edom. How would he react to the news that his supplanting brother had returned? Jacob sent messengers to break the news to Esau gently but these men returned with the distressing report that Esau was coming to meet his brother with four hundred armed men.

As his apprehension increased, Jacob sought the Lord in earnest prayer. Confessing that he was unworthy of the least of the Lord's mercies, Jacob asked for deliverance from the hand of his brother. After a season of prevailing prayer, Jacob sent gifts of his flocks and herds to Esau in hope of appeasing his brother's wrath. Then he rose up at night and sent away his wives and eleven sons for safety.

This left Jacob alone on the north bank of the brook Jabbok. It was dark, perhaps shortly after midnight. As Jacob returned to prayer, suddenly a man appeared in the inky darkness and attacked him. Jacob's first reaction must have been that this attacker was his brother Esau seeking revenge. Back and forth they wrestled and at first it seemed to be an even match. The wrestlers appeared to be equal in strength and skill so that neither

131

emerged victorious. The fight dragged on all night. Then, at *the breaking of the day,* the stranger touched the hollow of Jacob's thigh and it was thrown out of joint (Gen. 32:24-25). Suddenly Jacob realized that his antagonist was no ordinary man but the Angel Jehovah and that it was only God's grace and not Jacob's ability that the wrestling match had lasted as long as it did.

Over the years the Lord had been striving with Jacob. Yet the patriarch persisted in charting his own course, scheming, "wheeling and dealing" in order to be blessed. He was a man of a divided mind; he wanted to trust God and commit his life to Him but he wanted to rely on human devices as well. Jacob was miserable for he had not yet learned that an unsatisfied life results from an unsurrendered will.

When the light of day broke the wrestling match ended. Before Jacob would let the Lord go, however, he sought a reconfirmation of the blessing given him years before at Bethel. With Esau approaching it was important for Jacob to know that he was the heir of God. At this point the heavenly wrestler said, "Thy name shall be called no more Jacob, but Israel; for as a prince hast thou power with God and with men, and hast prevailed." Jacob had physically lost the wrestling match but had spiritually gained the victory. He had been emptied of his self-will, drained of his last effort to win in his own strength. Yet emptiness is the cup into which God pours blessing.

As the sun rose upon him, Jacob passed over Penuel, where he had seen God face to face, and discovered that he limped on his thigh. For the rest of his life he bore this physical reminder of that fateful wrestling match with the Lord.

When in prayer the Lord wrestles our will from us we may also bear some mark for the rest of our lives, but it will be worth it. One day in which our will is yielded to Him is worth a hundred years of striving to please Him in our own strength. "For it is God who worketh in you both to will and to do of His good pleasure" (Philippians 2:13).

MORNING HYMN
> *O Love that will not let me go,*
> *I rest my weary soul on Thee;*
> *I give Thee back the life I owe,*
> *That in Thine ocean depths its flow*
> *May richer, fuller be.*

Perfect Promises

MORNING SCRIPTURE   Joshua 6:1-27
MORNING VERSE   Joshua 6:15
And it came to pass on the seventh day, that they rose early about the dawning of the day, and compassed the city after the same manner seven times: only on that day they compassed the city seven times.

E very few years the countries of the free world participate in national elections. The democratic system of government provides the opportunity for men and women representing their parties to campaign, make promises and pledges, and run for office on the basis of their platform and promises. Generally the winner is the person who promises the most and who, in the minds of the voters, can actually deliver on those campaign promises. Unfortunately history has taught us that most political promises are little more than campaign rhetoric and the voters have justifiable reason for concern about their validity. In contrast to this are the promises of God in which the believer may have absolute confidence. God has a perfect record of keeping His promises.

The story of Jericho's conquest is a fine example of the completed promises of God. Prior to their entrance into the promised land, Joshua sent two men across the Jordan to spy out the city of Jericho. These spies came to the place where information would freely flow among the men of the town. They entered the house of Rahab the harlot. Although the life of Rahab as a harlot was certainly not condoned by the Israeli spies, nevertheless apparently the Lord God had been working in the heart of Rahab. When the king of Jericho attempted to track down the two spies, Rahab hid them on her roof among the sticks of flax. She confessed her faith in Jehovah God saying "The LORD your God, he is God in heaven above, and in earth beneath" (Joshua 2:11). Because this woman aided His secret agents, God promised Rahab and her household salvation in the midst of the peril of her city.

God's battle plan for the defeat of Jericho was unconventional, to say the least. Joshua would command seven priests, bearing seven trumpets of ram's horns before the ark of the Lord, to march around the city walls in silence for seven days, once each day until the seventh. On the seventh day they would march seven times around the wall. Then amid the blast of the seven jubilee trumpets and the war cry of the people of God, the destruction of the stronghold at Jericho would take place.

The children of Israel did as God commanded. "And it came to pass on the seventh day, that *they rose early about the dawning of the day* and compassed the city after the same manner seven times" (Joshua 6:15). On the seventh circuit of the seventh day the people shouted and the walls of Jericho fell down flat. The army of Israel entered the city unhindered and utterly destroyed all that was in the city, with one notable exception—the household of Rahab. Because they obeyed the Lord explicitly, the people saw two great promises of the Lord performed on the same day. The city of Jericho, the strongest outpost of the Canaanite defenses, had been utterly destroyed as God had promised. Likewise Rahab and her household had been spared destruction, as God had promised.

But there is one final promise of God that can be seen in the conquest of Jericho. In verse 26 Joshua counseled the people, warning them, "Cursed be the man before the LORD, that riseth up and buildeth this city Jericho: he shall lay the foundation thereof in his firstborn, and in his youngest son shall he set up the gates of it." To show that God means business when He makes a promise, Joshua imprecated a solemn curse on anyone who would rebuild the now-destroyed Jericho. This curse was literally fulfilled in the fate of Heil, the Bethelite, who rebuilt Jericho in the reign of Ahab (about 925 B.C.). Heil's firstborn son, Abiram, died as he was laying the foundation for the rebuilding of Jericho. Also his youngest son, Segub, died while he was setting up the gates of the city (1 Kings 16:34). What God promises, God performs.

Whether the promise is for salvation, as in the case of Rahab, or for destruction, as in the case of Heil, the promises of God must never be taken lightly. Whatever God promises, God performs. You can count on it.

MORNING HYMN
> *Standing on the promises that cannot fail,*
> *When the howling storms of doubt and fear assail*
> *By the living word of God I shall prevail,*
> *Standing on the promises of God.*

Friendship

MORNING SCRIPTURE   2 Samuel 16:1–17:24
MORNING VERSE   2 Samuel 17:22
*Then David arose, and all the people that were with him, and
they passed over Jordan: by the morning light there lacked not
one of them that was not gone over Jordan.*

One of the prize gems of human relationships is friendship. Emerson said, "The only way to have a friend is to
be one," an echo of Proverbs 18:24. Friendship always
enriches our lives, but sometimes it preserves them as well. The
friendship of Hushai with David is a fine example.

Nathan's prophecy upon David for his great sin was severe
and swift in coming. It struck first with David's son Amnon,
and quickly thereafter with the hot-tempered Absalom.
Absalom's rebellion against his father had taken firm root in
Israel. He was clearly in command and was now residing in
Jerusalem. But the aura of David's presence in Israel and the
legend of his prowess as a man of war made Absalom's rebellion tenuous. He must pursue his own father and the warriors
who were with him. How would this be done?

Absalom's close advisor, Ahithophel, hatched a plan, the
sagacity of which was unrivaled. He proposed that the armies
of Israel pursue David with twelve thousand chosen men and
fall on him when David and his soldiers were weary and sapped
of strength. They would kill David only. What is most unbe-
lievable is that Absalom readily agreed that this was a good
plan. But in the providence of God, Absalom opted to get another opinion before he enacted it. Thus he called Hushai the
Archite. Although pretending allegiance to Absalom, Hushai
remained the loyal friend of David and acted as his informer
revealing Absalom's every move.

The plan of Hushai was a classic case of overkill. He called
for Absalom to gather Israel from Dan to Beersheba, as many as
the sand of the sea, against David in battle. His rhetoric must
have appeared venomous and thus Absalom liked the plan even
more than that of Ahithophel. The foolish Absalom did not know

that this plan was divinely originated and calculated for his own destruction. "For the Lord had appointed to defeat the good counsel of Ahithophel, to the intent that the Lord might bring evil upon Absalom."

No sooner was the plan accepted by Absalom than Hushai dispatched Zadok and Abiathar the priests to warn David of the impending danger. David arose and all his men passed over the Jordan River *by the morning light* (2 Samuel 17:22). They were taking no chances; they fled at the rising of the sun. It is always a wise decision to flee evil at the beginning of the day.

Absalom pursued his father across the Jordan River and the famous incident of catching his long-flowing hair in the boughs of a great oak tree occurred that day. That day Absalom was killed. God had crushed an evil rebellion against His ordained king through the loyalty and godly commitment of a friend.

Visitors to the Ft. Myers, Florida, home of Thomas Alva Edison, are intrigued by a path in his garden which he called "the walk of friendship." The uniqueness of this walk is that each of the stones which constitute the walk was given to Edison by a friend. The pathway is designed as a memorial to friendship, the kind of friend that Hushai was to David, for friends lead friends step by step out of danger into delight.

If you have a close friend, rejoice in that friend and thank God for him or her. Enjoy that bond of friendship which you have. In fact, why not write or call that friend today and tell him you love him in the Lord and are praying for him. You'll never know what it will mean to him if you don't.

MORNING HYMN

> *What a Friend we have in Jesus,*
> *All our sins and griefs to bear!*
> *What a privilege to carry*
> *Ev'rything to God in prayer!*
> *O what peace we often forfeit,*
> *O what needless pain we bear,*
> *All because we do not carry*
> *Ev'ry thing to God in prayer.*

Awake Early

MORNING SCRIPTURE   Psalm 108:1-13
MORNING VERSE   Psalm 108:2
Awake, psaltery and harp: I myself will awake early.

A re you a morning person? Do you know others who claim to be night people? If so, whether morning person or night person, each of us must ask ourselves if our heart is fixed upon God.

David wrote in Psalm 108, "O God, my heart is fixed; I will sing and give praise, even with my glory" Whether a morning person or a night person, the one who knows and loves the Lord God can have an unperturbed heart when he sees the world reeling around him. Our hearts bow to sing and give praise with all our intellect, our skills, our resources, ourselves. It is the call to obey the command of the unperturbed heart which causes us to rise in the morning with a song on our lips. David, an early riser, not only resolved to sing and give praises to God with his lips, but resolved to employ the use of musical instruments in that same melody of praise. He implores, "Awake, psaltery and harp." Not content with singing the praises of God alone, he will use the well-tuned strings of the psaltery and harp and his flying fingers to accompany his vocal chords.

Still, the key to his praise for God is not found in his voice or in the psaltery and harp. The key is found in his call to "awake" himself to the lively pursuit of praise to God. It is only when a thoroughly enraptured soul sings to God that his vocal praise is acceptable to Him. David says, "Awake, psaltery and harp: I myself will awake *early*" (Psalm 108:2). His praise to the Lord God will precede the dawn. The best and brightest hours of the day will find the psalmist heartily aroused to bless God. Not only will he awaken early to praise Him but he will awaken every fiber of his being to praise God. Some engage in praise to God in a halfhearted manner; these sing in drawling tones, as if they were half asleep. They arise early to praise God but do not awaken their minds, their spirits, and their bodies in praise to God. Early risers who seek to please the Lord must make certain that they have awakened themselves thoroughly before they begin to praise Him or their practice of predawn praise will be reduced to mere ritualism.

Having a time alone with God early in the morning is a blessed experience. But too often our prayer life early in the morning is burdened down with weariness, sleepiness, and a half-awake attitude toward God. When we have our morning devotions we must be certain that we are wide awake and ready to meet with God. Then will our meeting with the Almighty be something enjoyable, something vibrant, alive, and awake.

Henry Ward Beecher relates an incident about a laborer on his father's farm in Litchfield, Connecticut. Of this laborer he said: "He had a little room, in one corner of which I had a small cot, and as a boy I used to lie there and wonder at the enthusiasm with which he engaged in his devotions. It was a regular thing. First he would read the New Testament, hardly aware that I was in the room. Then he would alternately pray and sing and laugh. I never saw the Bible enjoyed like that! But I want to bear record that his praying made a profound impression upon me. It never entered my mind whether or not his actions were appropriate. I only thought, 'How that man does enjoy it!' I gained from him more of an idea of the desirableness of rejoicing prayer than I ever did from my mother or father. He led me to see that there should be real overflowing gladness and thanksgiving in it all."

Is it any wonder that when David's heart was fixed upon God he called himself to awaken early in praise of God. To have our minds ready, the psaltery and harp ready, but not ourselves ready is an affront to our early morning praise to God.

Let us always be alert, awake, and available to praise God early in the morning. Only as we are sufficiently alive to engage in a meaningful and enjoyable prayer life with God will He hear us when we pray, "Be thou exalted, O God, above the heavens, and Thy glory above all the earth."

MORNING HYMN
Oh, the pure delight of a single hour
That before Thy throne I spend,
When I kneel in prayer, and with Thee, my God,
I commune as friend with friend!

Fleece or Faith

MORNING SCRIPTURE   Judges 6:16-40
MORNING VERSE   Judges 6:38
And it was so: for he rose up early on the morrow, and thrust the fleece together, and wringed the dew out of the fleece, a bowl full of water.

Discouraged and pathetic Israel needed a champion. God had chosen His man   The angel of the Lord appeared unto Gideon, a mighty man of valor, and encouraged him with the promise of God's presence and power. Gideon had broken down the altar to Baal. Idolatry throughout the land of Israel was pounded with a heavy blow. Jehovah alone was now worshiped in Ophrah and the fame of Gideon spread throughout the land. It was apparent that Gideon was the man behind whom all Israel could rally.

Once again the Midianite Bedouins swarmed across the land. Gideon knew that the time for battle had come, but this time he was ready. Judges 6:34 says, "The Spirit of the LORD came upon Gideon," literally, the Spirit of Jehovah clothed Gideon like a garment. The once discouraged and despondent young farmer of Ophrah was now suited up for battle in the armor of the Spirit of God. When he sounded the mustering trumpet, immediately all of the clan of Abiezer gathered around him. Messengers were sent throughout all the land. From Naphtali, Zebulun, Asher, and Manasseh they came, prepared to fight under the leadership of Gideon.

All was ready for the mighty battle, yet one thing more troubled Gideon. Again he asked a sign from the Lord. Seeking a sign from God was characteristic of Jewish behavior (1 Corinthians 1:22). With troops arrayed for battle, Gideon spread a fleece of wool on the ground and said to the Lord God, "If the dew be on the fleece only, and it be dry upon all the earth beside, then shall I know that Thou wilt save Israel by mine hand, as Thou hast said." A heavy dew is very common in the highlands of Palestine. Even today clothes left outdoors overnight must be wrung out in the morning. Although energized for

139

battle, the entire camp of Israel waited throughout the night for the sign from God.

The Scripture records that Gideon *rose up early on the morrow,* and wrung enough dew out of the fleece to fill a bowl full of water (Judges 6:38). Miracle accomplished! However, Gideon entreated the grace and patience of the Lord again and asked Jehovah to reverse the sign. One more night the Israelites waited before entering battle. In the morning the ground was saturated with dew but the fleece was entirely dry. This was proof positive that God was in this battle and that Gideon was His chosen leader

Frequently much indecision and lack of courage is camouflaged under the guise of "putting out the fleece." Such a practice is not always an admirable one, nor does it always produce admirable results. When John Wesley was a thirty-two-year-old missionary in Georgia he fell deeply in love with a young woman he wanted to marry. Some of his friends suggested that perhaps God would have the evangelist remain unmarried and devote his life to his work. One even suggested they draw lots in order to discern God's will for Wesley. The evangelist agreed. Three small slips of paper were prepared: one said, "Marry"; the second, "Think not of it this year"; and the third, "Think of it no more." Wesley drew a slip and with much sadness read, "Think of it no more." Heartbroken, he ended his courtship. Fifteen years later Wesley married a wealthy widow who became a hindrance to his ministry. After twenty years of mutual misery, she left him. He had allowed a fleece to determine his fortune.

When God sets up the parameters, encourages us in a given situation, and calls us to action, let's not be guilty of "fleecing" Him. How much better if Gideon had been remembered for his faith, as was Abraham, than for his fleece. For what will you be remembered?

MORNING HYMN
> I am trusting Thee, Lord Jesus
> Trusting only Thee;
> Trusting Thee for full salvation, Great and free.
> I am trusting Thee to guide me,
> Thou alone shalt lead,
> Ev'ry day and hour supplying All my need.

Incomplete Obedience

MORNING SCRIPTURE   1 Samuel 15:1-35
MORNING VERSE   1 Samuel 15:12
And when Samuel rose early to meet Saul in the morning, it was told Samuel, saying, Saul came to Carmel, and, behold, he set him up a place, and is gone about, and passed on, and gone down to Gilgal.

Incomplete obedience is the half brother of disobedience. Not to obey God explicitly is to disobey Him implicitly Saul is an example of this kind of disobedience.

Several great military victories over Moab, Ammon, Edom, and the kings of Zobah all strengthened Saul's position as king of Israel and secured for him the loyalty of the people. He was their hero, and he was beginning to know it.

Still, the great Bedouin tribe of the Amalekites continued to harass the Jews. In the past, at Sinai, in the wilderness, and in the days of Gideon, these Amalekites repeatedly attacked the Israelites without provocation. Thus, through the prophets, God told Saul to kill the wicked Amalekites and destroy all their livestock. He wanted His people to realize just how much He hates sin and thus God would not allow them to be enriched in any way by the conquests of their ungodly neighbors.

Mustering a force of two thousand infantrymen and an additional ten thousand men from Judah, Saul marched to the south against the Amalekites. Saul's victory over the Amalekites was complete and decisive. The Israelite army annihilated the entire tribe as God had commanded. But Saul did something that God did not command, in fact, something He explicitly prohibited. "And he took Agag the king of the Amalekites alive...and the people spared Agag and the best of the sheep and of the oxen, and of the fatlings, and the lambs, and all that was good, and would not utterly destroy them."

Twice before Saul had shown himself unfit for leadership because of his disobedience to God. Now God indicated to Samuel that Saul could no longer be king because of his disobedience and rebellion; he would be rejected by God. So distressing was this news to Samuel that he cried unto the Lord all night long, but to no avail. Jehovah's mind was set; Saul must go. Reluctant to deliver such a message to the king and having wrestled about it with God all night, Samuel *rose early* to meet Saul *in the morning* (I Samuel 15:12).

When Samuel approached Saul at Gilgal, Saul piously greeted him, "Blessed be thou of the LORD," as if he had done nothing wrong. In fact he reported, "I have performed the commandment of the LORD." But Samuel knew otherwise and pointedly asked the king, "What meaneth then this bleating of the sheep in mine ears, and the lowing of the oxen which I hear?" Bleating sheep and lowing oxen are seldom informers, but in this instance they revealed the partial disobedience of the king, demonstrating again the principle of Numbers 32:23, "Be sure your sin will find you out."

Embarrassed that his disobedience had been discovered, but always ready with an explanation, Saul violated his leadership and squarely blamed the people for this sin. Samuel rehearsed in Saul's ears what the Lord had commanded him to do and how he had failed to keep the Lord's command. Assuming that the prophet would be pacified by the prospects of a sacrifice to Jehovah, Saul thought he had devised the perfect excuse for disobedience. How could God not be pleased with a sacrifice? But Samuel countered, "Hath the LORD as great delight in burnt offerings and sacrifices, as in obeying the voice of the LORD?" There was no answer. Saul was trapped in his disobedience.

The lesson that Saul failed to learn is one that we must not fail to learn from him. Samuel taught the king, "Behold, to obey is better than sacrifice." Obeying the voice of God can never become subservient to acts of worship or service. Obedience is the primary response necessary from a servant to his master. Partial obedience merely betrays rebellion against our master and thus partial obedience is in reality disobedience. First, last, and always obedience is the very best thing.

MORNING HYMN
> *When we walk with the Lord In the light of His Word,*
> *What a glory He sheds on our way!*
> *While we do His good will He abides with us still,*
> *And with all who will trust and obey.*

Prayer and Peace

MORNING SCRIPTURE   Isaiah 26:1-21
MORNING VERSE   Isaiah 26:9
With my soul have I desired Thee in the night; yea, with my spirit within me will I seek Thee early: for when Thy judgments are in the earth, the inhabitants of the world will learn righteousness.

One of the prevailing themes of both Old and New Testaments is the constant presence of peace in the hearts of those who abide in God. The prophet Isaiah said it this way, "Thou wilt keep him in perfect peace, whose mind is stayed on Thee: because he trusteth in Thee" (Isaiah 26:3). Literally Isaiah said, "Thou wilt keep him in peace, peace" or, God will keep us in double peace, He will give us a double portion of peace when our minds rest on Him.

Likewise in the New Testament Jesus taught His disciples that His very presence would bring them peace. He said, "Peace I leave with you, My peace I give unto you: not as the world giveth give I unto you" (John 14:27). He told His disciples, "These things I have spoken unto you, that in Me ye might have peace. In the world ye shall have tribulation: but be of good cheer; I have overcome the world" (John 16:33).

The Apostle Paul understood the principle of fixing our minds on God and enjoying His peace. He counseled the Colossian believers to "let the peace of God rule in your hearts, to the which also ye are called in one body; and be ye thankful" (Colossians 3:15). If our minds are stayed upon God, His peace will rule the affairs entertained by our minds. If, on the other hand, we allow our minds to dwell on the cares of this world, God's peace will be far from our thoughts.

It is for this very reason that the apostle told the Philippian believers, "Be careful for nothing" or, be full of care about nothing "but in everything by prayer and supplication with thanksgiving let your requests be made known unto God. And the peace of God, which passeth all understanding shall keep your hearts and minds through Christ Jesus" (Philippians 4:6-7). The peace of God which garrisons our hearts and minds cannot exist alongside of the cares of this life. Each of us must make the decision whether our minds will dwell on those things that trouble us or on the power of God to deliver us. A mind full of care can be a mind full of peace. The difference is only a prayer away.

Isaiah was in the habit of seeking God in the middle of the night. When the thick clouds of sorrow overshadowed his heart and he no longer could endure the disappointments of that day, he did not allow his mind to dwell on those disappointments but rather on the Lord's deliverance. Rather than lay his head on a pillow of doubt, he would lay it on the pillow of dependence on the Lord God.

Isaiah continued, "Yea, with my spirit within me *will I seek Thee early*" (Isaiah 26:9). The experience of meeting the Lord in the darkness of midnight and having his mind freed from fear enabled the prophet to face the new day eagerly awaiting an additional measure of God's peace. Thus he determined that his spirit would seek the Lord early, fully confident that the Lord would answer his prayer: "Lord, Thou wilt ordain peace for us: for Thou also hast wrought all our works in us" (Isaiah 26:12).

The pattern for dealing with the cares of this world is the same for us today. God has designed us to live at peace with Him, with our world, and with ourselves. But we can do this only as we turn our cares over to Him in exchange for His ruling peace. Whatever difficulties you faced yesterday and wrestled with through the night last night, give them early this morning to the Lord and let Him replace your cares with the comfort of His peace. Remember, God's peace is but a prayer away.

MORNING HYMN

> *Peace! peace! wonderful peace,*
> *Coming down from the Father above;*
> *Sweep over my spirit forever, I pray,*
> *In fathomless billows of love.*

Reasonable Service

MORNING SCRIPTURE   Exodus 24:1-18
MORNING VERSE   Exodus 24-4
And Moses wrote all the words of the LORD, and rose up early in the morning, and builded an altar under the hill and twelve pillars, according to the twelve tribes of Israel.

C onsecration to the Lord requires separation from evil, devotion to God, and the endless pursuit of holiness. Although the Lord would have all His children be fully consecrated to His service, He requires of us "reasonable" service (Romans 12:1). Consecration made under the influence of emotion or the excitement of the moment is not to be trusted. The believer must carefully, prayerfully, and reasonably count the cost of discipleship before committing his life in service to the Lord.

After the great law was given to Moses on Mount Sinai, God sought ratification of the covenant He had made with the Israelites. Once again Moses ascended the holy mountain, this time with Aaron, Nadab, Abihu, and seventy of the elders of Israel. When they descended again, Moses relayed to the people all the ordinances of God's covenant. As soon as the terms of the covenant were known, "the people answered with one voice, and said, All the words which the LORD hath said will we do" (Exodus 24:3). Immediately Moses sensed that the people were too readily consecrating themselves to the ordinances of God's covenant and had not counted the cost. Thus Moses maneuvered to make their consecration more reasonable.

First Moses purposefully prolonged the process of consecration. He did not permit the people to ratify the covenant at once. Instead, this great man of God wrote down all the words of the Lord and went to bed. He *"rose up early in the morning,* and builded an altar under the hill, and twelve pillars, according to the twelve tribes of Israel"* (Exodus 24:4). The altar was built in preparation for the sacrifice without which no covenant was considered binding. By making the people wait one day before they could officially ratify the covenant, Moses reduced the emotional influence of the Israelites' hasty acceptance of the covenant.

Secondly, Moses surrounded the ratification of the covenant and the consecration with impressive ceremonies. He sent the young men, perhaps the firstborn of the families since the Levitical order had not yet been instituted, and they offered burnt offerings and sacrificed peace offerings of oxen unto the Lord. This was to be a solemn occasion, one which the Israelites would not soon forget.

Thirdly, great pains were taken to insure that the people understood the terms of the covenant. They could not properly consecrate themselves to God if they did not fully comprehend what their consecration meant. Not only did Moses relay the words of the Lord to the people when he descended from the mountain, but now, a day later, he read from the book of the covenant in the hearing of all the people. Moses wanted to be absolutely convinced that the people were making a rational decision to give their lives in service to the Lord.

Finally, Moses took the blood of the sacrifice and sprinkled it on the people saying, "Behold the blood of the covenant, which the LORD hath made with you concerning all these words." It was the blood which sealed the covenant. It was the symbol of the covenant. The blood of the sacrifice was placed upon the people to etch in their minds that they were chosen of God and now consecrated to Him.

Choosing a life of consecration to the Lord should be a sensible, reasonable, thoughtful act. The decision to give yourself to God and His service is a solemn act based in reason, not in emotion. It is indeed praiseworthy for a believer to consecrate his life to the Lord, but he must never do so lightly or thoughtlessly Before committing your life in service to God today, count the cost, for "No man, having put his hand to the plough, and looking back, is fit for the kingdom of God" (Luke 9:62).

MORNING HYMN
All for Jesus, all for Jesus!
All my being's ransomed pow'rs:
All my tho'ts and words and doings,
All my days and all my hours.

The Gift of Criticism

MORNING SCRIPTURE   John 8:1-32
MORNING VERSE   John 8:2
And early in the morning He came again into the temple, and all the people came unto Him; and He sat down, and taught them.

It was after a church service one morning in which the minister had preached on spiritual gifts that he was greeted at the door by a lady who said, "Pastor, I believe I have the gift of criticism." The pastor looked at her and asked, "Remember the person in Jesus' parable who had the one talent?" The woman nodded her understanding. "Do you recall what he did with it?" "Yes," replied the lady, "he went out and buried it." The pastor suggested, "Go, thou, and do likewise!"

The Pharisees and Sadducees apparently felt they too had the gift of criticism. Frequently they attempted to ensnare the Lord Jesus. As was the Master's habit, He entered Jerusalem crossing the Mount of Olives and *"early in the morning* He came again into the temple, and all the people came unto Him; and He sat down and taught them"* (John 8:2). His reappearance in the Temple provided an opportunity for the Pharisees and scribes to lay a subtle snare for Him. They brought a woman taken in the very act of adultery. The Feast of Tabernacles had just been celebrated and acts of immorality during that festive week were not unusual. The scribes attempted to put Christ in a dilemma by quoting the law of Moses. They knew that if He answered that the woman should be stoned, He would violate the Roman law which forbade such acts. However, if Jesus answered that the woman should not be stoned, He would be violating Moses' law (Deuteronomy 22:24).

The religious leaders were not so much interested in the adulterous woman as they were in Jesus' response to her situation. Their criticism of her was motivated by their desire to entrap Him. But Christ knew well how to repel such attacks by an appeal to higher principles. The same law which adjudged the guilty to be stoned to death also required the witnesses to cast the first stones. Jesus' statement, "He that is without sin among you, let him first cast a stone at her," was sure to bring an end to their criticism. The crowd, one by one, stealthily left the scene. Ironically enough, the only one who was left was the Lord Jesus, the only one of the crowd who had lived a perfect life and had a right to condemn her.

This very teaching is reiterated by the Apostle Paul in Romans 8. Paul asks the hypothetical questions, "What shall we then say to these things? If God be for us, who can be against us?...who shall lay anything to the charge of God's elect? It is God that justifieth. Who is he that condemneth? It is Christ that died, yea rather, that is risen again, who is even at the right hand of God, who also maketh intercession for us" (Romans 8:31, 33-34). Only the mind of God could conceive of a plan whereby the one person who lived a righteous life and had the right to condemn us was the very person who laid down that life to die for us. The woman taken in adultery was speaking to the one who did not come into the world to condemn the world, but to save the world.

One businessman keeps a fairly large stone on his desk. The stone is mounted and lettered with one word, "First." This acts as a constant reminder to him of Jesus' words, "He that is without sin...let him first cast a stone." When his employees enter his office and there is reason to criticize them for their lack of achievement, the man looks at the stone and recalls his own shortcomings. He deals with his employees in mercy and grace.

This passage of Scripture does not teach us to look the other way when people sin. It does not teach us that we ought to condone adultery or any other crime. What it does teach us, however, is that it is not the responsibility of a Christian continually to be on the lookout for sin in other Christians, or anyone else for that matter. If we have lived a perfect life, we can be a watchdog on others who have not lived a perfect life. But we have enough trouble keeping ourselves in line; we need not constantly be critical of the way others live. Jesus was teaching the critical religious leaders of His day that, although the woman was a great sinner, she was no greater a sinner than they were. We must remember the same as we meet others today.

MORNING HYMN
More like the Master I would live and grow,
More of His love to others I would show;
More self-denial like His in Galilee,
More like the Master I long to ever be.

Glory to God

MORNING SCRIPTURE   Judges 7:1-25
MORNING VERSE   Judges 7:1
Then Jerubbaal who is Gideon, and all the people that were with him, rose up early, and pitched beside the well of Harod: so that the host of the Midianites were on the north side of them, by the hill of Moreh, in the valley.

N atural man has a penchant for trying to explain away God. The theory of evolution was developed in an attempt to remove God from the arena of creation. Liberal theologians have attempted to demythologize the Bible in order to remove the miraculous works of God from it. Man does all he can to explain naturally the divinely originated phenomena in our world.

God has always been aware of man's desire to usurp His position and authority Frequently in Scripture can be found accounts where God places men in deliberate situations so they must recognize their deliverance is solely of Him. When God removes the possibility of any natural explanation, man is left with the inevitable conclusion that God is in the miracle business. Such was the case in our Scripture today.

Israel was assembled and ready for battle. Already the fight had been stayed two days by the dewy and dry fleece so that Gideon could receive a token of God's presence with them. Now the fight was to be delayed again.

On the morning following the second test with the fleece, Gideon and all the people with him *"rose up early* and pitched beside the well of Harod"* (Judges 7:1). Anxious for the battle, they had already moved into military position when God told Gideon he had too many people in His army. Jehovah wanted to be certain that Gideon, as well as Israel and the nations watching, would understand that Israel had won the battle by the hand of God. Therefore he instructed Gideon to command any of the thirty-two thousand troops who were afraid to return home from the front. Much to the surprise of Gideon, twenty-two thousand admitted their fear and retreated. Surely if a battle were won by ten thousand Israeli troops against one hundred thirty-five thousand Midianites (Judges 8:10) this would indicate that the victory was the Lord's. But again Jehovah surprised Gideon by indicating that these ten thousand troops were still far too many.

Gideon was to take the troops to the spring of Harod for a strange and severe test. The soldiers were divided into two groups, those who lapped water as a dog and those who dropped to their knees to drink. Whatever the purpose of the test, only three hundred soldiers were selected for Gideon's army.

Next God instructed Gideon to go with his servant Phurah down to the perimeter of the Midianite encampment and eavesdrop on the Midianites. They overheard one soldier telling another of his dream about a cake of barley bread that rolled into the Midian camp against the king's tent and flattened it. His fellow soldier interpreted the dream that this was none other than the sword of Gideon and that God was about to deliver Midian into Gideon's hands. So evident was it that this dream and the interpretation had both come from God that Gideon immediately returned to the host of Israel and said, "Arise; for the LORD hath delivered into your hand the host of Midian." Three hundred men defeated the entire Midianite army and the glory belonged entirely to God.

We must never shy away from impossible situations. When the odds seem least favorable for our success, that is when God can gain the greatest glory from our success. Large armies are not as admirable as dedicated ones. The recruiting slogan of the United States Marine Corps is "A few good men." God is looking for the same. Will you be one today?

MORNING HYMN

> On ev'ry hand the foe we find
> Drawn up in dread array;
> Let tents of ease be left behind,
> And onward to the fray!
> Salvation's helmet on each head,
> With truth all girt about:
> The earth shall tremble 'neath our tread
> And echo with our shout.

Morning Moments

MORNING SCRIPTURE   Psalm 119:129-152
MORNING VERSE   Psalm 119-147
I prevented the dawning of the morning, and cried; I hoped in Thy word.

Today our early morning devotional takes us to the great psalm—Psalm 119. This is a psalm dedicated to the praise of God's Word. It is the longest and most elaborate of the alphabetic psalms. While there are eight other acrostic psalms (9; 10; 25; 34; 37; 111; 112; and 145), this one far exceeds all the others in splendor. It is arranged in twenty-two stanzas, corresponding to the twenty-two letters in the Hebrew alphabet. Within each stanza the first line of every verse begins with the same letter in the Hebrew alphabet. Although we cannot see that in English, in our Bible the word supplied at the head of each stanza is the name of the Hebrew letter with which each verse in that stanza begins.

The author of the psalm is unknown but it is definitely Davidic in tone and expression and squares with David's experiences at many interesting points.

While these details of the psalm are interesting, devotionally there is something far more important in Psalm 119. The Masseretes, those scribes who copied the ancient Hebrew manuscripts of the Old Testament, observed that in every verse but one (verse 122) there is a direct reference to the law under one of ten legal names found in the psalm. Others dispute that claim but it is clear that the theme of this great psalm is the Word of God. The great preponderance of verses contain at least one word which identifies the Word of God and sings man's praises to it.

Psalm 119 is filled with delightful expressions of appreciation for God's Word. "Wherewithal shall a young man cleanse his way? By taking heed thereto according to Thy word" (verse 9). "I have rejoiced in the way of Thy testimonies, as much as in all riches" (verse 14). "I will speak of Thy testimonies also before kings, and will not be ashamed" (verse 46). "For ever, O LORD, Thy word is settled in heaven" (verse 89). "Thy word is a lamp unto my feet, and a light unto my path" (verse 105). With

151

expressions of love and devotion like these, what more could God hear that would bring joy to His ears? What promise could the psalmist make that would seal his eagerness to know God's law?

Psalm 119:147 provides the answer. The psalmist says, "I prevented the dawning of the morning, and cried; I hoped in Thy word." Before the light broke through the shadows of the dark night, the psalmist was already prevailing on God in prayer. He cried unto His God before He spoke unto his fellow man. He spent time hoping in God's Word each morning before he gave himself to speaking God's Word throughout the day. It was at the dawning of the morning that the psalmist found the Word of God most precious to him.

Ambrose commented, "It is a grievous thing if the rays of the rising sun find thee lazy and ashamed in thy bed, and the bright light strike on eyes still weighed down with slumbering sloth." The psalmist would agree with this church father.

To delight in the law of God, to sing praises to the Word of God, to read and meditate on the testimonies of God, all bring joy to the heart of God. But I believe the greatest joy is brought to His heart when we do these things at the dawning of the day. When we seek His word above all others, His encouragement before all others, His truth instead of all others, then we will be pleasing to Him more than all others.

One grand benefit of preceding the dawn with Bible reading and prayer is that it will not only add God's blessing to our day, but it will also encourage us to continue in His Word and prayer throughout the day. The same psalmist who rose early in the morning to hope in God's Word continued into the night watches meditating in that same Word (verse 148). When we begin the day early in prayer and the Word, we can continue that practice throughout the day. But if we do not come to the Lord until the evening hours, we can never know the joy of spending the day with Him. Let us enjoy His Word throughout this day.

MORNING HYMN
> *Break Thou the bread of life, Dear Lord, to me,*
> *As Thou didst break the loaves, Beside the sea;*
> *Beyond the sacred page, I seek Thee, Lord;*
> *My spirit pants for Thee, O living Word.*

Come and Dine

MORNING SCRIPTURE   John 21:1-25
MORNING VERSE   John 21:4
*But when the morning was now come, Jesus stood on the shore:
but the disciples knew not that it was Jesus.*

Have you ever noticed that the most difficult time to serve the Lord is immediately after a defeat in your life? When we are on a spiritual high, serving the Lord comes almost naturally. But when we experience the roller-coaster ride to the depths of despair after some spiritual tragedy we have a tendency to become complacent. While activity tends to produce additional activity, inactivity also reproduces itself.

The popularity of Jesus Christ had been building throughout His earthly ministry. Thousands of people followed Him through the hills of Galilee, watching His miracles and listening to His teachings. The disciples had become an intimate group, well known for their association with Jesus. As His popularity grew, so did their own.

The culmination of their intimate relationship with the Lord came the night of His betrayal. He had gathered the disciples in the upper room to keep the Passover. They were all there. They ate with the Lord, prayed with Him, sang hymns with Him, pledged their loyalty to Him. Around this meal, the institution of the Lord's supper; the disciples reached a spiritual high. Their heightened spirits, however, were soon to be dashed. Jesus was led away from the garden, He endured a cruel and illegal trial, and the disciples were dispersed. Even though Jesus again and again had told them that He must suffer the cruelty of the cross, the disciples still did not assimilate this tenet of His teaching. With His death and burial the disciples' balloon had burst. Even the resurrection of the Lord and the immediate post-resurrection appearances did not do much to reassure the disciples.

As instructed by the Lord Himself, the disciples returned to Galilee. Their meeting with Jesus on the mountain of Galilee where He had appointed them must have been subsequent to the account of our Scripture for today. Seven of the apostles had returned to their vocation as fishermen. How easy it was to be a follower of the Lord when He was present; how easy it was to return to their occupation in His absence.

It was Peter who first suggested that he would go fishing. This does not necessarily imply that he intended to renounce his apostleship in favor of the fishing trade. This is what he knew best; this is what he would do until the Lord commanded him otherwise. Hence Peter and the others entered into a ship and fished all night, but caught nothing. How could this be? Had they lost the knack of fishing during their years with the Messiah? Why were they so unsuccessful at a business in which they had been extremely successful before Jesus called them to discipleship? Throughout the night they fished without any success at all.

"But when the morning was now come, Jesus stood on the shore" (John 21:4). For some providential reason the disciples did not recognize the stranger standing on the shore. As He called to them inquiring how successful they had been, they had to answer that they were extremely unsuccessful in fishing that night. They did not recognize that it was the resurrected Lord keeping His rendezvous with them in Galilee until He commanded them to cast their nets on the other side of the ship. This was reminiscent of a similar but earlier command of the Lord with the same result (Luke 5:1-11).

When the disciples hauled in an incredible amount of fish, they came to the shore at Jesus' invitation to "Come and dine" (John 21:12). It was almost as if the Lord was reigniting the fire of intimacy and love which had cooled since their last supper together. Jesus Christ did not want His disciple band to become complacent, for complacency is kin to disobedience.

After we have once served the Lord well and lived in intimate relationship with Him, it is easy to become complacent, to drift from Him, and not to sit at His table. However, the Lord calls to each of us to "come and dine" and if we are to be an effective and useful tool in the Master's hand we must find our feet under His table frequently.

MORNING HYMN
> *Revive us again—fill each heart with Thy love;*
> *May each soul be rekindled with fire from above.*
> *Hallelujah, Thine the glory! Hallelujah, amen!*
> *Hallelujah, Thine the glory! Revive us again.*

Little Things

MORNING SCRIPTURE   1 Samuel 17:1-27
MORNING VERSE   1 Samuel 17:20
And David rose up early in the morning, and left the sheep with a keeper, and took and went, as Jesse had commanded him; and he came to the trench, as the host was going forth to the fight, and shouted for the battle.

Occasionally it is necessary to remind ourselves that success in life often depends upon little things. Little people, little tasks, and little responsibilities often loom large in the eyes of God.

The Philistines waged frequent raids on Israel. The leader of the Philistines, a giant of tremendous stature named Goliath of Gath, was probably one of the Anakim (Numbers 13:33; Joshua 11:22), a strain of huge men that Joshua drove out of Hebron, and who took refuge among the Philistines. No Israelite was a match for Goliath, especially not little David who was sent to the battlefield to inquire of the welfare of his three elder brothers, Eliab, Abinadab, and Shammah. David's task was a small one; he was entrusted with very little. Told to take his brothers an ephah of parched corn and ten loaves, along with ten cheeses for the captain of the army, David set out to the battlefield. This day began with a small task, but it was to be a most momentous day in the history of Israel.

"David *rose up early in the morning,* and left his sheep with a keeper" and engaged in the small chore his father had commissioned to him (1 Samuel 17:20). As he talked with his brothers, behold the Philistine champion came out again to challenge the Israelites. The armies of Israel stood by trembling in their sandals, but David was appalled and amazed at the fear which paralyzed the Israelite warriors. Not willing to see his nation shamed or his God embarrassed, he inquired why someone did not stand up to the godless Goliath. "Who is this uncircumcised Philistine, that he should defy the armies of the living God?" Immediately his eldest brother whisked him away to quiet him. Someone entrusted with such a small task as bringing bread and

155

cheese to his soldier-brothers should not be so vocal about the cowardice of the Israelite army.

Yes, David had slain the lion and the bear, but he was still slight in the sight of those around him. Those were but small feats; silencing the giant Goliath would be a gargantuan task. Besides, even if David accepted the challenge, he was too small to wear the armor necessary to enter battle with Goliath. His weapon, a sling, was likewise a small implement. Everything about David was small, including his chances of success against the giant. But as we all know, David's God was victorious; the slight shepherd of Israel slew the giant Goliath.

Horatius Banal; reflecting on God using that which is small, realized that little things can frequently be used of God to be great things. He wrote, "A holy life is made up of a multitude of small things. It is the little things of the hour and not the great things of the age that fill up a life like that of the Apostle Paul or John, or David Brainard, or Henry Martyn. Little words not eloquent speeches or sermons, little deeds not miracles or battles, or one great heroic effort or martyrdom, make up the true Christian life. It's the little constant sunbeam, not the lightning, the waters of Siloam that go softly in their meek mission of refreshment, not the waters of the rivers great and main rushing down in torrent, noise, and force that are the true symbols of the holy life."

There are no small people, small tasks, or small responsibilities in the service of God. You can be small only if you fail to take the bread and cheese as God has commanded. How much happier Goliath would have been if little David had stayed home that day.

MORNING HYMN
> *Little is much, when God is in it!*
> *Labor not for wealth or fame;*
> *There's a crown—and you can win it,*
> *If you'll go in Jesus' name.*

Praising God

MORNING SCRIPTURE   1 Chronicles 23:1-32
MORNING VERSE   1 Chronicles 23:30
And to stand every morning to thank and praise the LORD, and likewise at even.

K ing David, who himself had been a fugitive and a wanderer for many years of his life, would have liked nothing better than to build a permanent dwelling place for the ark of the covenant. But because he was a man of war, Jehovah would not permit David to realize this privilege, so David "called for Solomon his son, and charged him to build an house to the LORD God of Israel" (1 Chronicles 22:6). The zealous David did all he could to help in the preparations for the building of this Temple. He gathered materials, prepared iron for nails, and had a crew of masons readied. But an even greater contribution than arranging for the materials may have been David's initiation of the first full choral service. In conjunction with the chief of the Levites, David set apart three families and commissioned them to the service of the Temple. These were not just singers but prophets as well, "to prophesy with harps, with psalteries, and with cymbals" (1 Chronicles 25:1). Generation after generation their instruction was handed down from father to son and their art and musical skill was carefully perpetuated.

These families were those of Asaph, the son of Berechiah the Gershonite, the chief singer and also a distinguished seer; of Heman the Kohathite, the grandson of the prophet Samuel and himself, "the king's seer in the words of God" (1 Chronicles 25:5); and of Jeduthun (or Ethan), a Merarite, who is also called "the king's seer." Each of the names of these leaders is found in the titles or superscriptions of selected psalms in the Psalter.

From 1 Chronicles 23-25 we learn that the numbers of Levites involved in the service of the Temple and Tabernacle was enormous. The three families numbered two hundred eighty-eight principal singers, divided into twenty-four courses of twelve each. The total number of Levites engaged in the important task of praising Jehovah with the instruments which

David made was four thousand. Six thousand were designated as officers and judges, four thousand were set apart to be door-keepers, and the remaining twenty-four thousand Levites were designated to the general "work of the house of Jehovah."

Although to us their work may appear to be mundane, it certainly was not to them. They were to wait on the priests for the service of the house of Jehovah, purifying the holy place and the holy things, preparing the shewbread and the meat offering, and assisting in the offering of burnt sacrifices on the sabbaths and on feast days. But perhaps their greatest duty, as well as their greatest delight, was "to stand *every morning* to thank and praise the Lord and likewise at even" (1 Chronicles 23:30).

Rising early in the morning these Levites would initiate the praise to Jehovah that day. This was not only a responsible position but a very meaningful one as well. Psalm 88, a psalm for the sons of Korah designated as a Maschil of Heman, gives a fine example of what these Levites may have said morning after morning in praising Jehovah. "But unto Thee have I cried, O LORD; and in the morning shall my prayer prevent [come before] Thee" (Psalm 88:13).

Rising early in the morning to initiate a day filled with praise to God is our privilege as well. May we be as faithful in exercising that privilege as David's choirmasters were. Faithfulness in early praise to God may make the difference between a good day and a bad day.

MORNING HYMN
> *Holy, Holy, Holy, Lord God Almighty!*
> *Early in the morning our song shall rise to Thee;*
> *Holy, Holy, Holy! Merciful and Mighty!*
> *God in Three Persons, blessed Trinity!*

Believing Is Not Seeing

MORNING SCRIPTURE   Isaiah 37:1-38
MORNING VERSE   Isaiah 37:36
Then the angel of the LORD went forth, and smote in the camp of the Assyrians a hundred and fourscore and five thousand: and when they arose early in the morning behold, they were all dead corpses.

"N ow faith is the substance of things hoped for, the evidence of things not seen" (Hebrews 11:1). Perhaps no more graphic illustration of this truth can be found in the Scriptures than the events recorded in Isaiah 36 and 37. The Assyrian king, Sennacherib, had opened a campaign against Judah by attacking the fortresses in her southland. He was engaged in the siege of Lachish, a city southwest of Jerusalem, when he decided to send a contingent of soldiers against Jerusalem under Rabshakeh, his chief cupbearer. Apparently the Assyrians felt that King Hezekiah would surrender Jerusalem without a fight if Rabshakeh could dishearten the Jewish warriors.

The Assyrian cupbearer made light of Judah's possibilities of victory. Would she rely on the armies of the Pharaoh of Egypt, armies now so weakened that they are likened to leaning on a broken staff? Would she rely on the God of Israel in the face of the might of Assyria? What would Hezekiah and his Israelites do? The servants of King Hezekiah came to seek advice from Isaiah, the man of God. Isaiah assured Hezekiah that God took the blasphemies of Rabshakeh as uttered against Him personally and would destroy the armies of Sennacherib because of their blasphemy. In destroying the armies of the Assyrians the whole world would know "that Thou art the LORD, even Thou only" (Isaiah 37:20). Isaiah predicted that the king of Assyria would never enter God's holy city nor shoot an arrow at it. God would somehow miraculously deliver His city because of the blasphemy of the Assyrians against Him. Hezekiah and the Jews must live lives of faith for they would not be told how this deliverance would come about; they must trust God.

That very night the predicted catastrophe for the Assyrian armies occurred. "Then the angel of the LORD went forth and smote in the camp of the Assyrians a hundred and fourscore and five thousand: and when they arose *early in the morning*, behold, they were all dead corpses" (Isaiah 37:36). God had kept His word, even though the Jews could not see through the fog of doubt. Early in the morning they arose to find one hundred eighty-five thousand Assyrian corpses. They never had opportunity to move against God's holy city because God always performs what He promises.

On July 4, 1952, Florence Chadwick attempted to swim from Catalina Island to the California coast. It was not the distance that was the great challenge to her but the bone-chilling waters of the Pacific. To make mattes worse, a dense fog enshrouded the entire area, making it impossible to see the land. After she had swum for fifteen hours and was within half a mile of her goal, Florence Chadwick gave up. Later she told a newspaper reporter, "If I could have seen land, I might have made it."

Not long thereafter she again attempted this same feat. Once again the fog shrouded the coastline and she could not see the shore, but this time she successfully completed her swim because she kept reminding herself that the land was out there, somewhere. With that confidence she bravely swam on and achieved her goal. In fact, she broke the men's record by more than two hours.

Sometimes we do not achieve our goals in life because we cannot clearly see God's hand moving in our behalf. Although we desire with all our heart to reach our goal, the fog of doubt sets in and makes it impossible for us to see clearly. Still, if believing in God we continue to press toward the mark, early in the morning we will see our goal achieved and the battlefield littered with the corpses of the enemy. We must trust God in the dark; we must remember that faith is the evidence of things not seen.

MORNING HYMN

> *O for a faith that will not shrink*
> *Tho pressed by many a foe,*
> *That will not tremble on the brink*
> *Of any earthly woe.*

Joy in the Morning

MORNING SCRIPTURE   Psalm 30:1-12
MORNING VERSE   Psalm 30:5
For His anger endureth but a moment; in His favour is life: weeping may endure for a night, but joy cometh in the morning.

L ike in so many other psalms, in Psalm 30 David promises to praise the Lord. He had experienced a great deliverance and was thankful. He cried unto Heaven and the Lord heard him, bringing his soul back from the grave. Thus he exclaims that he will "Sing unto the Lord...for His anger endureth but a moment." This thought is reinforced by the delightful expression, "Weeping may endure for a night, but joy cometh *in the morning*" (Psalm 30:5).

How often have we experienced the truth of this verse! Heavy trials weigh us down as we pillow our heads at night. Our minds seem unable to bear the pressure. Restlessly we toss and turn, but our body refuses to rest. We are miserable and feel helpless. Finally sleep comes, but only after hours of restlessness.

The Christian life is filled with the interchanges of sickness and health, weakness and strength, disgrace and honor, want and wealth. Sometimes we enjoy the comfort of being one of God's own; other times we bear the cross of that same privilege. On occasion the south winds of God's mercy blow over our lives; on other occasions blow the north winds of adversity. Nonetheless, when the nipping north winds of calamity chill our nights and cause us to be restless, we may rest in the promise of God that "weeping may endure [only] for a night." God always places a time limit on the suffering and restlessness of His children.

After such a night of struggle, we frequently awake with a vague sense of what transpired the night before. As we gather our thoughts, we wonder why it was so difficult for us to fall asleep. Why were we so helpless and despairing? Things do not look as impossible as they once did. What is it that makes the difference? It is the joy which comes in the morning when we cast our care upon the Lord knowing that He cares for us (1 Peter 5:7; cf. Job 33:26; Isaiah 26:20; 54:7).

Not only are the trails of the night temporary; they are gifts from God as well. We cannot deny that Christians are often called to endure soul-shaking experiences. In the Christian life there is weeping, and sometimes plenty of it. The nights of adversity are long and frequent. But God never allows them to be endless or without cause.

The cupola of St. Paul's Cathedral in London was painted by Sir James Thornhill. It was necessary for Sir James to complete his work while standing on a swinging scaffold high above the pavement. One day when he had finished a particularly difficult portion with painstaking effort, he stopped to inspect his artistry. As a good artist does, slowly he began moving backwards in order to gain a more appropriate view of his work. A helper working with him suddenly recognized that Sir James, should he take one step further backward, would be killed in a fatal fall. The man knew that if he startled the man with a shout it might topple him from the scaffold. Thus, as quickly as possible, he grabbed a brush and made a sweeping stroke across the exquisite work that Sir James was admiring. Understandably disturbed, the artist rushed forward with a cry of dismay. When his companion explained why he had taken this drastic measure, Sir James Thornhill burst into tears of gratitude.

We may be sure that no physician ever weighed out medicine to his patients with half as much care and exactness as God weighs out the trials of a sleepless night to us. Perhaps the dawning light of relief seems far away for you, but remember, morning will come, and with it God's promised joy. You have God's Word on it.

MORNING HYMN
> *Does Jesus care when my heart is pained*
> *Too deeply for mirth and song,*
> *As the burdens press, and the cares distress,*
> *And the day grows weary and long?*
> *O yes, He cares; I know He cares,*
> *His heart is touched with my grief;*
> *When the days are weary, the long nights dreary,*
> *I know my Saviour cares.*

Web of Conspiracy

MORNING SCRIPTURE   Judges 9:22-57
MORNING VERSE   Judges 9:33
*And it shall be, that in the morning, as soon as the sun is up,
thou shalt rise early, and set upon the city: and, behold, when he
and the people that is with him come out against thee, then mayest
thou do to them as thou shalt find occasion.*

O h what a tangled web we weave, when first we practice
to deceive." Conspirators against those who are righteous are ultimately destroyed by their conspiracy. How
this is evident in the tragic days following the triumph of Gideon
and his three hundred men.

Judges 8:33-35 records the failure of the Israelites to live
after the defeat of the Midianites as they had during the battle.
As a result of Israel's forgetting the God who delivered them,
internal strife became more damaging than their external enemies. The royalty which Gideon had refused was coveted by
Abimelech, his son by a handmaiden of Shechem. Attempting
to trade on his father's reputation, Abimelech harangued the
men of Shechem, claiming that it was far better to be ruled by
one man, a Shechemite, than by all seventy of Gideon's sons.
With money stolen from the sacred treasury of Baal-berith,
Abimelech hired "vain and light persons," a band of despera-
does, to slay Gideon's other sons. Miraculously, however, one
son, Jotham, escaped the conspiracy.

Abimelech reigned over a limited area in Israel for three
years. But his reign did not go unchallenged by Jotham, who
fled to Mount Gerizim where he pronounced a curse on
Abimelech and the men of Shechem. This curse came in the form
of a parable about the tree which wished one of their number to
rule over them. They asked the olive tree, fig tree, and vine in
succession, only to be rebuffed each time. Then they turned to
the worthless thorny bramble, which accepted their offer to rule
over them.

The meaning of this parable was obvious to all. The trees,
which are themselves producers, are more interested in fruit
than in control; but the thorn, which has nothing to give, seeks

to be the leader sheerly for personal gain. Abimelech was a thorn. Jotham cried, "Let fire come out from Abimelech and devour the men of Shechem, and the house of Millo; and let fire come out from the men of Shechem, and from the house of Millo, and devour Abimelech"(Judges 9:20).

Jotham's curse was not long in being fulfilled. After three years God sent an "evil spirit" between Abimelech and the men of Shechem. The Shechemites revolted and plotted against his life. But Zebul, the governor of the city and an Abimelech loyalist, informed Abimelech of the plot to dethrone him and a counter plan was hatched. Zebul counseled Abimelech and his men to lie in wait for the Shechemites during the night in the fields before the city. "And it shall be, that in the morning, as soon as the sun is up, thou shalt rise early and set upon the city"(Judges 9:33). Abimelech massacred the inhabitants of Shechem.

Having treacherously murdered his pseudosubjects, Abimelech turned his attention to the neighboring city of Thebez. As some of the Shechemites, the men and women of Thebez fled to a strong tower for safety. Again Abimelech prepared to burn them out when a woman cast a piece of millstone out of the tower. In ironic reciprocation, the stone found its target—the head of Abimelech—and broke his skull. Jotham's prophecy was fulfilled.

Abimelech, the would-be-king conspirator, and the Shechemites, his would-be subjects, were caught in the middle of their web of conspiracy. Having destroyed the righteous, they were themselves destroyed by each other. Deception always brings destruction. How much better we are passively to accept the will of God as good, acceptable, and perfect (Romans 12:2) than to conspire self-promotion without the blessing of God.

MORNING HYMN

> *The God of Abraham praise,*
> *Who reigns enthroned above,*
> *Ancient of everlasting days*
> *And God of love.*
> *Jehovah, great I AM,*
> *By earth and Heav'n confessed,*
> *I bow and bless the sacred*
> *Name forever blest.*

God Alone

MORNING SCRIPTURE   Job 7:1-21
MORNING VERSE   Job 7:4
When I lie down, I say, When shall I arise, and the night be gone?
And I am full of tossings to and fro unto the dawning of the day.

The book of Job is an epic poem ranking among the greatest writings of mankind. Alfred Lord Tennyson said that the book of Job was "the greatest poem of ancient or modern times." As the story of a man who lived righteously before God, was fiercely attacked by Satan, continued his righteous life, and had restored to him all that he lost and more, Job ought to be an encouragement to all of us. Somewhere in the book you and I find ourselves.

It was not bad enough that Job was attacked by Satan, but his three friends, who sought to comfort him, were equally vicious in their pompous assumptions about Job's sin. The majority of Job's chapters record cycles of speeches given by Job's friends and the replies of the righteous Job.

The first cycle contains the speech of Eliphaz. In vivid language, Eliphaz describes a vision in which he saw the majestic purity of God compared with the sinfulness of all of God's creative beings. Since only the evil perish, Job was experiencing his difficulty because he was evil, Eliphaz thought. His suggestion was that the righteous Job not be bitter but turn to God in repentance.

In replying to Eliphaz, Job likens human life to service in the armed forces, to the life of a hireling, to the lowly lot of a servant. Job can identify with each of these roles for he too is caught in a life situation well beyond his control. He recognizes that the servant or hireling has but a few days on earth and many of these days are lived in menial meaninglessness. Job feels the same way about his life, now that his family and possessions are gone and his friends have turned against him, assuming his unrighteousness.

I suppose each of us has had occasion to identify with Job 7:4. When Job lies upon his bed at night, and sleep does not come, his only thought is, "When shall I arise, and the night be gone?" When financial reversals or personal loss plague us and faithful friends fail us, the nights do seem long indeed. Like Job, we may feel that we are "full of tossings to and fro *until the dawning of the day*" (Job 7:4).

What can Job do? Where can he turn? Who is the one person who will listen and understand? In the transitoriness of life, who remains the same and forever? Job knows the answer; he will make his prayer to God and there find his hope.

Vance Havner once told a story about an elderly woman who was disturbed by her great and many troubles. Some of these troubles were real, others were but imaginary. After friends and family had prayed with her, comforted her, and attempted to help her, they reminded her, "Grandma, we've done all we can for you. You'll just have to trust God for the rest." With a look of shock and despair Grandma's eyes flashed back to her family the message, "Oh dear, has it come to that?" Havner notes, "It always comes to that, so we might as well begin with that!"

This is the lesson that Job learned. Sometimes in attempting to provide comfort, our family and friends actually do a disservice to our need. Sometimes we are misunderstood for our actions. But God always understands and God is always a source of comfort. It always comes to the need of resting in God. We may rest in Him for our health and strength, for vindication from false accusations, for companionship in time of solitude. It always comes to that and thank God it does.

MORNING HYMN
> *When peace, like a river, attendeth my way,*
> *When sorrows like sea billows roll—*
> *Whatever my lot, Thou hast taught me to say,*
> *It is well, it is well with my soul.*

Failure and Success

MORNING SCRIPTURE   Joshua 8:1-35
MORNING VERSE   Joshua 8:10
*And Joshua rose up early in the morning. and numbered the people,
and went up, he and the elders of Israel, before the people of Ai*

I t has been aptly said that failure is the back door to success. Nowhere is this adage more graphically illustrated in Scripture than in the capture of Ai. With a task force of three thousand men, Israel had failed miserably in her attempted conquest of Ai because of one man's sin. Achan kept God's people from victory, but once his sin had been dealt with, victory would most assuredly come again to Israel.

The defeat at Ai could have dealt a devastating blow to Joshua's leadership. Joshua feared the Canaanites would hear of Israel's cowardice and their name would be cut off from the earth. His concern really was what such a defeat would mean to the great name of Jehovah God. But his fears were alleviated when Jehovah promised Joshua victory in the second battle of Ai.

The plan of attack for this battle, unlike that of Jericho, was far more likely to be included in military manuals. God told Joshua to put an ambush of thirty thousand men between Ai and Bethel to the west. To this was later added another ambush of five thousand men in the same direction. Meanwhile, "Joshua *rose up early in the morning,* and numbered the people, and went up, he and the elders of Israel before the people of Ai" (Joshua 8:10). When the king of Ai saw what was happening, he too "hasted and *rose up early*" in the morning (Joshua 8:14). Mustering his Aiite troops, they marched out to meet the main body of the Israelite forces. Because the enemy was fully aware that Israel had retreated once in defeat, Joshua feigned a retreat, drawing his troops back to the northeast. The Aiite troops followed.

While this was happening, the Israelites waiting in ambush entered the now empty city of Ai and burned it to the ground. When the king and his men turned to see their city smoldering, they realized their defeat was imminent. They were surrounded by Israelite soldiers. The Israelites in the ambush then came out of Ai and marched on the rear flank of the Aiite army. Joshua reversed his movement and caught the king and his men in a pincer movement. The people of Ai were defeated; Joshua's victory was now complete.

Joshua had taken the stumbling stone of defeat and turned it into the stepping-stone of success. In doing so he learned the valuable lesson that our greatest glory consists not in never failing, but in rising every time we fall. Others give striking testimony to this fact as well.

In 1832 a young American was a candidate for the legislature. He lost. In 1834 he was again a candidate and this time won. In 1847 he went to the United States Congress but served only one term. He wasn't even renominated by his party. He campaigned for Zachary Taylor for president, hoping to be appointed commissioner of the General Land Office. He wasn't. He returned to private law practice. In 1854 he again ran for the legislature and won but soon resigned because he hoped the new anti-Nebraska party would support him for the senate. They didn't. In 1856 he was nominated for the office of vice-president of the United States and lost. In 1858 he ran again for United States senate and lost again. In 1860 he was simply nominated as a favorite son from Illinois for the presidency— and later that year he, Abraham Lincoln, was elected president of the United States. Like Lincoln, we must never allow yesterday's mistakes to bankrupt tomorrow's efforts.

Just as there is no failure more disastrous than success that leaves God out of the picture, likewise there is no success greater than the rediscovery of the power of God in our life. We must never be ashamed to confess that we have failed, for this is but one way of saying we are wiser today than we were yesterday

MORNING HYMN
Immortal, invisible, God only wise,
In light inaccessible hid from our eyes,
Most blessed, most glorious, the Ancient of Days,
Almighty, victorious—Thy great name we praise.

The Deceitful Heart

MORNING SCRIPTURE   Exodus 32:1-35
MORNING VERSE   Exodus 32:6
And they rose up early on the morrow, and offered burnt offerings, and brought peace offerings; and the people sat down to eat and to drink and rose up to play.

T he prophet Jeremiah observed that, "The heart is deceitful above all things, and desperately wicked; who can know it?" (Jeremiah 17:9). The Bible gives more than ample evidence to support Jeremiah's observation. In fact, so does this morning's newspaper.

A prime example of how innately wicked the human heart is can be seen in the unfaithfulness of Israel at Mount Sinai. When the people of God encamped at the foot of the mountain, Moses ascended the slopes of Sinai and received the Law. After the people acknowledged the covenant of God and answered with one voice, "All the words which the LORD hath said will we do" (Exodus 24:3), Moses again ascended the mount of God. This time he received God's instruction in the ordinances of divine worship.

Moses' sojourn on the mountain was much longer than anyone expected. After nearly six weeks passed without his return, the people grew impatient and fearful. Had they lost their leader? How could Moses survive on the mountain without food? And what about their God? He was on the mountain too, in the pillar of cloud that led them from Egypt. Had He forsaken them?

Israel had come face to face with a real test of faith, a test they failed miserably. As long as Moses was with the Israelites he could encourage them to "live by faith and not by sight." But now he was gone and Israel's faith rapidly evaporated. The desperate wickedness of their hearts came to the fore. The Israelites frantically begged Aaron to make gods for them, gods that would go before them as the Everlasting God had done in the cloud. Immediately Aaron instructed the people to take off their golden earrings, which were then melted down and fashioned into an idolatrous golden calf. Aaron proclaimed that on the next day they would have a feast to the Lord.

The Israelites were like a child with a new toy, barely sleeping that night because of excitement. "And they *rose up early on the morrow*, and offered burnt offerings and brought peace offerings" (Exodus 32:6). The people then sat down to eat and drink. But the Bible says that after that they "rose up to play." This may sound innocent enough, but the "play" in which the people of God engaged was hardly the harmless kind. They fell into the pattern of sensuality that accompanies pagan worship. Idol worship nearly always ended in an orgy so disgusting that it cannot be described. So boisterous was the Israelite orgy that when Moses and Joshua returned from the mount, Joshua assumed the delirious shouts of the people were noises of war. But the people of God were caught up in a wild frenzy which was both licentious and idolatrous. It was the sight of this frenzy that angered Moses and caused him to cast the tables of stone to the ground, breaking them.

Exodus 32:25 enhances our understanding of the depths to which the Israelites had fallen. Not only were the people worshiping an idol engaged in a wild orgy, and worked into a frenzy by licentious dancing, they were naked as well. Their nakedness was not only offensive to Moses but it was an affront to God as well.

There is scarcely a depth to which Satan cannot drag the desperately wicked human heart, even the hearts of God's chosen people. New Testament believers must never be deceived into thinking that we have sufficient strength in ourselves to keep us from similar depths of sin. Only the Spirit of God can prevent our wicked hearts from dragging us into sin. Today, let us pray as the Lord Jesus taught us, "And lead us not into temptation, but deliver us from evil" (Matthew 6:13).

MORNING HYMN
> *Search me, O God, and know my heart today;*
> *Try me, O Saviour, know my thoughts, I pray;*
> *See if there be some wicked way in me:*
> *Cleanse me from ev'ry sin, and set me free.*

Rewardable Service

MORNING SCRIPTURE   Matthew 19:16–20:16
MORNING VERSE   Matthew 20:1
For the kingdom of heaven is like unto a man that is an householder, which went out early in the morning to hire labourers into his vineyard.

Jesus' favorite method of teaching was by parable. A parable is an account which may or may not have actually happened but nonetheless is designed to teach a truth. One of our Lord's most difficult parables is the parable of the kingdom which is likened to a householder.

In summary the parable is this. *Early in the morning* one day a householder went out to hire laborers for a vineyard (Matthew 20:1). He agreed to pay the laborers a penny for the day, which was evidently the regular wages for the ordinary laborer About the third hour the man returned to town and hired others to work in his vineyard, promising to pay them what was fair. At the sixth, ninth, and eleventh hours he returned to find others standing idle and likewise hired them with the same promise of payment.

At the end of the day, the householder called his laborers together and had the steward of the house pay them, beginning with the last hired. Each was paid the same, but when those who were hired early in the morning received just a penny they murmured that it was unfair to pay them a penny when those who had worked only an hour were also paid a penny. The householder replied that he had been just with the daylong workers, as he had been with the hourlong workers, and that whatever funds he had were his; he could do with them as he chose.

What would the Lord have us to learn about Him from this parable? There are three things.

First, the Lord Jesus seeks laborers for His vineyard. There is much work to be done if we are going to win the world for Christ and train those who have been won to reproduce themselves and bear fruit in abundance. We are not saved to sit, soak, and sour; we are saved to serve the Lord. The most frustrated person in the world, I believe, is not the unsaved person; he has little understanding of what really awaits him. The most frustrated person in the world is the one who is saved and does not know why God has left him on the earth. Ephesians 2:10 claims, "For we are His workmanship, created in Christ Jesus unto good works, which God hath before ordained that we should walk in them." The Lord saved us to be laborers in His field.

Secondly, the Lord Jesus hires laborers at various hours and various stages in life. The Church did not begin fully equipped. Throughout history others have been added to the New Testament Church, as we have been added during these last decades. Those who were apostles in the New Testament Church will not receive a greater wage for their labors simply because they entered early into Christ's vineyard. God is interested in rewardable labor, not the hour in which we became laborers. Should you have come to know the Lord as Saviour later in life and not have the opportunities to serve Him as those who have been saved many years, do not despair. God is absolutely just in meting out rewards.

Thirdly, the Lord Jesus rewards generously as well as justly. This final lesson that this parable teaches us is perhaps the greatest of all. Each of these laborers was rewarded in an unexpected manner. Each one received a penny, a day's wage, and no one could complain that he was paid less than fair wages. Beyond acting justly to those who had been hired first, the householder acted generously to the others. When people see generosity to others and not to themselves, they are hurt and accuse the generous person of being unfair. But this is not the case. Having rewarded justly, the Lord Jesus was then free to reward generously.

A kind storekeeper once said to a little girl who was eagerly eyeing a jar of candy, "Take some; take a whole handful!" The little girl hesitated for a moment and then replied, "Will you please give it to me? Your hand is bigger than mine!" When we begin to compare our lives with others and compute our anticipated rewards, we will be dissatisfied. What we must do is let the hand of God reward us as He deems just and fair. Remember, His hand is always bigger than ours. Let us live for Him today; let Him reward us tomorrow

MORNING HYMN
> *Praise the Saviour, ye who know Him!*
> *Who can tell how much we owe Him?*
> *Gladly let us render to Him*
> *All we are and have.*

Jealousy

MORNING SCRIPTURE   1 Samuel 20:11-42
MORNING VERSE   1 Samuel 20:35
And it came to pass in the morning, that Jonathan went out into the field at the time appointed with David, and a little lad with him.

The wise Solomon once said, "Jealousy is cruel as the grave; its coals thereof are coals of fire" (Song of Solomon 8:6). The classic case of jealousy in the Bible is that of King Saul.

Young David had slain the giant Goliath and the women of the city responded by chanting, "Saul hath slain his thousands, and David his ten thousands" (1 Samuel 18:7). Hearing this displeased the king greatly. Saul was tormented by the thought that, although he was king over all Israel, yet the darling of the nation was David. Envy and jealousy, like a green-eyed monster, began to swallow him up.

No longer could David serve in the court of Saul, for twice Saul attempted to take his life. So David hid himself in the field and absented himself from the king's table. When the jealous Saul demanded of Jonathan the cause of David's absence, Jonathan's reply was that David had asked permission to attend a family feast at Bethlehem. But Saul saw this as merely an excuse and was enraged at his son. With the deepest insult possible to Jonathan, a slur with regard to his birth, Saul taunted the lad about his friendship with David. Ordered to fetch David so that Saul might kill him, Jonathan immediately reacted unfavorably and Saul hurled his javelin at his own son. Jonathan left the table in understandable anger.

"And it came to pass *in the morning*, that Jonathan went out into the field at the time appointed with David, and a little lad with him" (1 Samuel 20:35). Under the guise of target practice, Jonathan took the young lad to fetch his arrows as he shot them. This would prohibit Saul or anyone else being suspicious about why Jonathan was out in the field. When the young lad was dismissed, David emerged from his hiding place and the two lifelong friends renewed their covenant of friendship. Amid embraces and tears, they parted to meet again on only one brief occasion. This sad parting was occasioned by the jealousy of one man. Such jealousy removes the mind from reality and dethrones reason from its seat of judgment. The reins of reason are handed over to passion and the end result is illogical behavior.

D. L. Moody related a fable of an eagle who was envious of another bird that could fly better than he. One day the bird saw a sportsman with a bow and arrow and said to him, "I wish you would bring down that eagle up there." The man said he could do it if he only had some feathers for his arrow. So the jealous eagle pulled out one of his wing feathers. The man placed it on his arrow and shot at the flying eagle, but it did not quite reach the rival bird. The jealous eagle pulled out another feather, and another—until he had lost so many feathers that he could not fly himself. The wise archer then took advantage of the situation, simply turning around and killing the helpless bird at his side. Moody's application was simple: if you're envious of others, the one you will hurt the most will be yourself.

Saul's jealousy of David was his eventual undoing. Proverbs 14:30 says, "A sound heart is the life of the flesh; but envy the rottenness of the bones." We must never allow ourselves to fall prey to the monster within us, a monster that can arise on any occasion if we feed our jealousy.

MORNING HYMN
Would you live for Jesus and be always pure and good?
Would you walk with Him within the narrow road?
Would you have Him bear your burden, carry all your load?
Let Him have His way with thee.

Firm in Faith

MORNING SCRIPTURE   Mark 16:1-20
MORNING VERSE   Mark 16:2
*And very early in the morning the first day of the week they came
unto the sepulchre at the rising of the sun.*

F aith is not always a champion which marches alone. Sometimes faith is accompanied by fear. Faith is not the absence
of questioning, it is the presence of action in the midst of
those questions. Faith does not provide all the answers; it provides a basis for confidence in the midst of unreasonable circumstances.

We do not fully understand how God takes oxygen and hy-
drogen, both of them odorless, tasteless, and colorless, and com-
bines them with carbon, which is insoluble, black, and tasteless,
to produce a beautiful, white, sweet substance we call sugar.
Although we do not have all the answers as to how God accom-
plishes this, in the midst of our circumstances we accept God's
product on faith. Real faith is "the substance of things hoped
for, the evidence of things not seen" (Hebrews 11:1). Faith is trusting God when you cannot see through the fog.

It was early Easter Sunday morning when Mary Magdalene,
Mary the mother of James, and Salome set out on a mission of
faith. These women had covenanted among themselves to purchase spices that were needed to embalm the body of Jesus. They
could not do so until after dusk on Saturday. So, when the Sabbath was passed, the women purchased the sweet spices that
they might come to the tomb of Joseph and there make ready
for burial the body of the Lord Jesus.

It was *very early in the morning* the first day of the week that
they came to the sepulcher, *at the rising of the sun* (Mark 16:2).
With the spices in hand that they had purchased the previous
evening, the women made their way through the dark streets of
Jerusalem just before the sunrise of Sunday morning. As they
approached the garden in which the tomb was located, they chat-
tered among themselves questioning how they would gain ac-
cess to the tomb. Here is a grand example of faith amid questions. The women could not themselves roll away the stone for

it was simply too cumbersome to do so. Yet they did not stay at home and attend a seminar on stone-rolling, argue the pros and cons of gaining entrance to the tomb, or form a committee to study the problem. In the midst of their concerns about how they would gain entrance to the tomb, they steadily progressed toward the tomb in faith. Faith is not the absence of questions; it is the presence of action amidst those questions.

Once an ocean liner was engulfed in a dense fog off the coast of Newfoundland. It was Wednesday evening and the captain had been on the bridge for more than twenty-four hours when he was startled by someone tapping him on the shoulder. As he turned he saw the great man of prayer and faith, George Mueller. The concerned Mueller stated, "Captain, I must be in Quebec on Saturday afternoon." Expressing his dismay the captain replied, "That's impossible!" The fog was so dense and the progress of the ship so slow that the captain knew they would never make it to shore on time. He mumbled, "I'm helpless!" Being a man of faith, George Mueller suggested, "Let's go down to the chart room and pray." The captain, who could see only his circumstances, replied, "Do you know how dense the fog is?"

"No," Mueller said, "My eye is not on the density of the fog, but on the living God who controls every circumstance of my life." The captain and Mueller left the bridge and went below where Mueller fell to his knees and prayed. Within a matter of minutes the fog lifted, the ocean liner progressed rapidly, and Mueller was in Quebec before Saturday

If we are to live a life of faith we must get our eyes off the stone before the tomb and on the God who does the impossible. The women knew the stone would keep them from their Lord and yet they purchased their spices, readied themselves early in the morning, and made their way in the darkness toward the garden tomb. Faith is not being free from questions; faith is being firm in commitment to the power of God. How will you demonstrate your faith today?

MORNING HYMN

> *May Thy rich grace impart*
> *Strength to my fainting heart,*
> *My zeal inspire;*
> *As Thou hast died for me,*
> *O may my love to Thee*
> *Pure, warm and changeless be*
> *A living fire!*

Character

MORNING SCRIPTURE Psalm 73:1-28
MORNING VERSE Psalm 73:14
For all the day long have I been plagued, and chastened every morning.

This is the second psalm ascribed to Asaph, and the first of eleven consecutive psalms which bear his name. In 2 Chronicles 29:30 King Hezekiah invites the Levites to sing "the words of David, and of Asaph the seer." Asaph was not only a writer but a prophet as well. This psalm deals with the same perplexing subject as that of Psalm 37, curiously the transposition of Psalm 73. It is the subject of Psalm 49 and the entire book of Job. How can an infinitely powerful God be good and still allow the wicked to appear to prosper and the righteous to be in want? Perhaps you have asked the same question of God. If so, your answer is given in Psalm 73.

The way to Heaven is an afflicted way, a perplexed, a persecuted way, crushed close together with crosses as was the Israelites' way in the wilderness. This was true of Asaph the psalmist when his feet were almost gone and his steps had well nigh slipped. He was envious when he looked around him and saw the prosperity of the wicked. There were no pangs or pains in their death. The eyes of the wicked ever gloat on the luxuries around them. They increase in prosperity and riches while they curse God and the Almighty appears to do nothing about it.

On the other hand, Asaph had cleansed his heart and had washed his hands before God. He had lived uprightly and yet he was afflicted and distressed. Why would God allow him to be afflicted when he had lived as God desired? Although God does not daily bring a man to his bed, breaking his spirit and his bones, nevertheless seldom a day passes without some rebuke or chastening from God. It is as much a part of the Christian's life to know afflictions as it is to know mercies; to know when God smites as to know when He smiles.

Still Asaph complains, "For all day long have I been plagued, and chastened *every morning*" (Psalm 73:14). Every morning it appears to the psalmist that he arose after having been whipped by God. His breakfast was the bread of sorrow; his juice was the water of adversity. Morning after morning he would arise only to feel the affliction of God that day. Asaph began to question whether or not it was worth living a godly life, a life pure and unspotted from the world, when those around him refused to do so and prospered. Perhaps this question has crossed your mind as well.

In the forests of northern Europe lives the ermine, a small animal which we know best for its snow-white fur. Instinctively the ermine protects its white coat lest it become soiled. European hunters often capitalize on this trait. Instead of setting a mechanical trap to catch the ermine, they find its home in the cleft of a rock and daub the entrance with tar. A chase ensues and the frightened ermine flees toward its home. When it arrives at the cleft of the rock, finding it covered with dirt, the animal spurns its place of safety. Rather than soil itself and its white fur, it courageously faces the hunters. That's character. To the ermine, purity is dearer than life itself.

Whenever those occasions arise that we feel we are being chastised by God unjustly and we are tempted to cast off our righteous lifestyle, let's remember the ermine. To keep ourselves "unspotted from the world" (James 1:27) should be as important to the Christian as life itself. Affliction tests character and character tested, with the right response, is character strengthened. Rejoice today that God loves you enough to afflict you.

MORNING HYMN
> *In the hour of trial, Jesus, plead for me;*
> *Lest by base denial I depart from Thee;*
> *When Thou see'st me waver, with a look recall;*
> *Nor thro' fear or favor suffer me to fall.*

Betrayal

MORNING SCRIPTURE   Judges 16:1-31
MORNING VERSE   Judges 16:2
And it was told the Gazites, saying, Samson is come hither. And they compassed him in, and laid wait for him all night in the gate of the city, and were quiet all the night, saying, In the morning, when it is day, we shall kill him.

Of all the judges God raised up to steer Israel through the most stormy period of her history, none is as remarkable or pathetic as Samson. Like Samuel the priest, he was a son of much prayer. The announcement of Samson's birth to Manoah, his father, was made by an angel of the Lord. Judges 13:24 sums up the potential for God found in the life of Samson when it says, "And the child grew, and the LORD blessed him."

As he grew strong and tall, and kept to the restrictions of the Nazarite vow placed upon him (Judges 13:5), it soon became evident that this man was going to be a champion in Israel. Early the Spirit of the Lord began to move upon him (Judges 13:25). Three times during his early life the Scriptures note that "the Spirit of the Lord came mightily upon him" (Judges 14:6,19; 15:14). As long as Samson kept the razor from his head and pride from his heart, Samson would perform mightily for God.

There is evidence, however, that early in his life Samson began to enjoy his strength and stature. Although it was strictly forbidden of the Israelites to take wives of the Philistines, nonetheless Samson saw a Philistine woman of Timnath and said to his father, "Get her for me; for she pleaseth me well" (Judges 14:3). Samson's subsequent antics against the Philistines caused a committee of three thousand men of Judah to approach him and question, "Knowest thou not that the Philistines are rulers over us?" (Judges 15:11). But Samson was enjoying the might of the Spirit of the Lord and with the jawbone of an ass slew a thousand Philistines. He continued to judge Israel in the days of the Philistines for twenty years.

It was evident that something must be done to stop this Israelite strongman and the men of Gaza hatched a plan. When Samson went to a harlot of Gaza, one of his frequent and pathetic follies, the men of Gaza compassed him about, closed the city gate around him, and waited for an opportunity to kill him. They said, *"In the morning, when it is day, we shall kill him"* (Judges 16:2). But as before, their attempts were foiled when Samson arose at midnight, removed the doors of the city gate and carried them to the top of the hill alongside Hebron. This Philistine plan to kill Samson had failed; another would follow.

For the third and final time Samson would betray his people by an illicit relationship with a Philistine woman. The lords of the Philistines bribed Delilah to entice Samson to tell her the secret of his great strength. Three times he allowed himself to be bound with green withes or new ropes and to permit seven locks of his hair to be woven to the beam of a loom. Each time the treacherous Delilah would suddenly announce, "The Philistines be upon thee, Samson," and in human strength he would free himself to ward off the enemy. Samson appeared not to resent Delilah's evident treachery but rather to have enjoyed flaunting his strength before the Philistine lass. Finally, wearied by her persistence, Samson "told her all his heart" and confided to her the secret of his great strength. As he slept she cut his hair; his strength left him. The Philistines took him down to Gaza, bound him with fetters, put out his eyes, and caused him to grind grain in the prison house.

The story of the man upon whom the Spirit of the Lord came mightily could have been much different. It ended in tragedy because Samson displayed a total disregard for the laws of God with regard to the Philistines. He appeared to flaunt his God-given strength in a humanistic manner and continually to flirt with sin and disaster. Instead of fleeing the treacherous and deceitful Delilah, Samson tried to outwit and impress her. Perhaps the saddest comment of this sad life is found in Judges 16:20 where the writer notes of Samson, "He wist not that the LORD was departed from him."

We must recognize that our abilities and opportunities are truly gifts from God and we must use them mightily and wisely in the Spirit of the Lord. If we do not, like Samson, the world will make sport of us and our God.

MORNING HYMN
O how the world to evil allures me! O how my heart is tempted to sin!
I must tell Jesus and He will help me, Over the world the vict'ry to win.

Foolish Vows

MORNING SCRIPTURE   Genesis 44:1-17
MORNING VERSE   Genesis 44:3
*As soon as the morning was light, the men were sent away, they
and their asses.*

A weatherman, certain that his prediction for fair weather would be fulfilled, said, "If it rains tomorrow, I'll eat my hat!" Such a lightly considered vow is an invitation to disaster for it is entirely possible that factors unknown to the weatherman may cause a downpour. The Bible gives many similar examples of foolishly made oaths (cf. Judges 11).

During the worldwide seven years' famine in the days of Jacob, the sons of the patriarch found themselves trapped by such a foolish vow. They had sold their brother Joseph into slavery and unknown to them he had risen to a position of great authority in the Egyptian government. With the supply of grain in Canaan exhausted, Jacob sent his sons to Egypt to buy grain. In Pharaoh's land the brothers purchased grain from Joseph, whom they did not recognize. After that grain was gone, they returned to Egypt to buy more.

When they came to Joseph the second time he invited them to dine and commanded the steward to fill the men's sacks with food and put their purchase money back in each sack. Also Joseph specifically instructed that his silver cup be placed in the sack of the youngest brother, Benjamin. *"As soon as the morning was light"* the brothers embarked on the long trek back to Canaan (Genesis 44:3). Before they had gone very far Joseph commanded the steward to overtake them and accuse the brothers of stealing his royal cup. This was not done to be vindictive but simply to test the loyalty and integrity of the brothers who had once sold Joseph into slavery.

As soon as the charge was leveled against the sons of Jacob they indignantly denied it. To think that this steward would accuse them of dishonesty. In order to intensify their claim of innocence and fully unaware that Joseph had planted the cup in Benjamin's sack, the brothers hastily vowed a vow: "With whomsoever of thy servants it be found, both let him die, and we also will be my lord's servants." Suddenly they were trapped. They had made an irrevocable oath which would enslave them and bring death to their father's favorite son. When the search was made and the cup was found in Benjamin's sack, the brothers tore their clothes in anguish and returned to Joseph, the Egyptian governor.

It was no sin to vow this vow, for the making of such oaths was entirely voluntary. However, after a vow was made it was sacredly binding (Deuteronomy 23:21). The Apostle Paul called upon God in making an oath (2 Corinthians 1:23; 11:31) and our Lord Himself did not refuse to answer when put under oath (Matthew 26:63-64). Yet the Lord Jesus refined the general thought of Scripture on vowing vows when He said, "Swear not at all; neither by heaven...Nor by the earth.... Neither shalt thou swear by thy head.... But let your communication be, Yea, yea; Nay, nay; for whatsoever is more than these cometh of evil" (Matthew 5:34-37).

This does not mean that we cannot vow a vow to God. Rather, by the time of the New Testament the practice of making hasty and unmeaningful oaths was common. Oriental conversation was sprinkled with expressions like, "I swear that...." This profaned the true meaning and sacred character of a vow and our Lord condemned the practice. Much better, said He, that others are assured that what you say is true by your personal integrity than by an unmeaningful oath.

It would be better to make no oath at all than to make one with no intention of keeping it (Ecclesiastes 5:5). Vows made with pure intentions and based on certain knowledge can bring great blessings. But those hastily made, like that of Jacob's sons, or those loosely used in ordinary conversation, are to be shunned by all who seek a life pleasing to God. Be careful what vows you make today! Be careful to keep those you have made!

MORNING HYMN
> *So shall my walk be close with God,*
> *Calm and serene my frame;*
> *So purer light shall mark the road*
> *That leads me to the Lamb.*

Mysterious Ways

MORNING SCRIPTURE   Numbers 22:1-35
MORNING VERSE   Numbers 22:13
And Balaam rose up in the morning, and said unto the princes of Balak, Get you into your land: for the LORD refuseth to give me leave to go with you.

T he famous English hymnist William Cowper once wrote, "God moves in mysterious ways His wonders to perform." Nowhere in the pages of Scripture is this more evident than in the story of Balak, the king of Moab, and Balaam, the false prophet of Pethor in Mesopotamia.

With the conquest of the Amorites, the people of Israel neared their goal, the promised land. They descended into the valley of Jordan opposite Jericho on the plains of Moab. Such a bold move by Israel aroused the Moabites. Seeing that Israel was too strong for him in the field, Moabite king Balak made a confederacy with the sheiks of Midian. But even the combined strength of Moab and Midian was of doubtful value in the face of mighty Israel. It was evident to Balak that supernatural help must be sought.

The prophet Balaam, son of Beor, was one of those who still retained some knowledge of the true God. It is obvious, however, that he practiced the more questionable arts of divination as well and in fact believed that Jehovah was simply one of many gods. He found it quite to his advantage to believe in all the gods of oriental society. The emissaries from Balak came to Balaam with a strange request. There was a people come out of Egypt who covered the face of the earth. They were a threat to the very existence of Moab, or so the Moabite king believed. If Balaam would curse the intruders, the emissaries were empowered to give him the rewards of divination.

Balaam consulted the God of Heaven as to the advisability of cursing the people who had come out of Egypt. The answer of Jehovah left no room for variant interpretations. "Thou shalt not go with them: thou shalt not curse the people: for they are blessed" (Numbers 22:12). Balaam *rose up in the morning* and reported to the princes of Balak that Jehovah had directly forbidden him to curse their enemy Israel.

When the princes returned to Balak with this unexpected news, the Moabite king was undaunted. He sent to Balaam more numerous and more honorable envoys. The king promised the prophet that he would promote him to very great honor and give him any desire of his heart. The greed of Balaam was too much for his loyalty to the God of Heaven and consequently he wavered in his stand against cursing Israel. Instead of resting confidently on the clear word of the Lord, Balaam hedged on that clarity in order to feed his lustful desire for fame and honor. Thus God gave him his desire and delivered him to the destruction that he courted. Despite the evident will of God to the contrary, Balaam *rose up in the morning,* and saddled his ass, and went with the princes of Moab" (Numbers 22:21).

This Old Testament account features the miraculous happening of a dumb animal speaking to his master in order that the plan of God might be fulfilled. But an even more mysterious way in which God moved to perform His wonders was that He chose a false prophet, one who thought more of himself than he did of God, to advance one of the greatest prophecies of the Old Testament. It was Balaam the son of Beor who brought the message of Christ in the book of Numbers. His messianic prophecy was, "I shall see Him, but not now: I shall behold Him, but not nigh: there shall come a Star out of Jacob and a Sceptre shall rise out of Israel, and shall smite the corners of Moab, and destroy all the children of Sheth" (Numbers 24:17).

No greater prophecy concerning the messianic kingdom can be found anywhere in Scripture and, in the mysterious plan of God, this prophecy came from the lips of a self-seeking prophet. We may never fully be able to understand the methods or motives of God, but we are not required to understand them, simply to trust them.

MORNING HYMN
> *Praise to the Lord,*
> *Who o'er all things so wondrously reigneth,*
> *Shelters thee under*
> *His wings, yea, so gently sustaineth!*
> *Hast thou not seen*
> *All that is needful hath been*
> *Granted in what He ordaineth?*

The Trial of Faith

MORNING SCRIPTURE   Job 24:1-25
MORNING VERSE   Job 24:14
*The murderer rising with the light killeth the poor and needy,
and in the night is as a thief.*

Throughout Job's long ordeal one concern continually raced through his mind. He was fully aware that all men are sinners and therefore are justly deserving of divine punishment. His concern was, however, that he had always dealt with sin in an open manner. He had sacrificed daily to the Lord God and had conducted his life in such a way that it was pleasing to God. Throughout the ordeal the so-called comfort afforded him by his three friends was generated by the belief that Job's suffering was the result of secret sin and that, if he would confess that sin, God would surely remove the suffering. Job, however, knew of no secret sin in his life and believed that his suffering must be due to his piety. Job's mind was characterized by bewilderment, not by the suppression of known sin.

Job's understanding of the foolish heart of man is theologically correct. He knows that sin can never be successfully hidden from God. So wicked is the heart of man that he will confiscate the property of the fatherless, deny charity to the poor, and as wild asses *rising with the light* they kill the poor and needy assuming that no one will discover their crime (Job 24:14). "*The morning* is to them even as the shadow of death" (Job 24:17) for the rising of the sun brings to light the wickedness in which they have been engaged throughout the dark hours of the night. Yet Job knows that he has not conducted himself in this manner. It is understandable that God would punish with affliction those who have lived in the way Job has described, but it is not understandable why the righteous should suffer in the same manner. Job was upright before the Lord; how could the Lord allow this to happen to him? A similar circumstance once occurred in the life of William Carey, the pioneer missionary to India. After his work was established, those who supported him in England sent a printer to assist him in the work. Together they began producing portions of the Bible for distribution in India. One day while he was away from his station a fire broke out and completely destroyed everything Carey had accomplished. The building, the presses, the Bibles, and worst of all the manuscripts, grammars, and dictionaries on which he had spent many years of his life were all burned and destroyed. When Carey returned, his servant met him and tearfully relayed the news of the dreadful fire. How would Carey react? Without a word of despair or anger, William Carey knelt and thanked God that he still had strength enough to do that work all over again. Immediately he began, not wasting his time or licking his wounds. Before Carey died, under the direction of the Spirit of God he had not only duplicated his earlier achievements, but produced far better grammars, dictionaries, and translations of the Scripture than the first time.

William Carey had learned what Job had learned. Disaster does not necessarily mean the presence of secret sin. Sometimes God allows the pious to suffer just as He allows the impious. It is the trial of our faith that worketh patience and without this trial the legendary patience of Job would not be such a comfort to us today.

May each of us view those disasters that enter our lives through the godly glasses of courage and patience. May our lives be free from known sin so that with Job we may say of the Lord, "But He knoweth the way that I take: when He hath tried me, I shall come forth as gold" (Job 23:10).

MORNING HYMN

I would be true, for there are those who trust me;
I would be pure, for there are those who care;
I would be strong, for there is much to suffer;
I would be brave, for there is much to dare.

Morning Marching Orders

MORNING SCRIPTURE   Psalm 143:1-12
MORNING VERSE   Psalm 143:8
Cause me to hear Thy lovingkindness in the morning, for in Thee do I trust: cause me to know the way wherein I should walk for I lift up my soul unto Thee.

In today's modern, rushing world, many of us have all we can do to get out of bed in the morning and get to work on time. Often our schedule appears to preclude the possibility of morning devotions. Yet under the old dispensation of the law, it was the duty of the priestly tribe of the Levites to rise at dawn and give thanks and praise the Lord (1 Chronicles 23:30). We are not under the dispensation of the law, but as New Testament priests (1 Peter 2:5,9) we too should begin the day with God. If we do, we will have a keen sense of His presence with us throughout the busy hours that follow.

This great truth was obviously known by David. One of the most enjoyable verses to come from his pen is Psalm 143:8, "Cause me to hear Thy lovingkindness *in the morning;* for in Thee do I trust: cause me to know the way wherein I should walk; for I lift up my soul unto Thee." In this morning prayer David made two requests: to hear the lovingkindness of God in the morning, and to know the way in which he should walk throughout the day. These two requests bear a definite relationship.

David wanted the lovingkindness of God to engage his thoughts and affections early in the morning. If other thoughts get into our hearts in the morning, we may not be able to burn them away throughout the day. Prayer and praise, reading and meditation will influence our minds for hours throughout the day. Lovingkindness is a favorite theme of David. Simply, lovingkindness is love that shows kindness. By deeds and words it is God living through us to a hurting world. That's the kind of life David wanted to live. The Lord's lovingkindness is our all-sufficient source of joy. Such joy can be sought elsewhere but found only here. It is the divine joy that sweetens every bitter experience of life and makes even those that are sweet, sweeter still. It binds every wound, and is the balm for every hurt. It is little wonder that David sought such an experience early in the morning. With that kind of start, what must the rest of the day be like?

The old expression is here very applicable, "Well begun; half done." David began his day well by seeking the Lord and His lovingkindness. Half the battle of a successful day was already won. He continued to ask the Lord to show him the way he should walk throughout the day. Frequently the path we determine to be logical for our daily walk is not the path designed by God. We must keep the same close touch with Him hour after hour that we began with Him in the morning.

Speaking of his mountain-climbing experience, nineteenth century preacher George Barrell Cheever commented on this verse: "The whole valley is surrounded by ranges of regal crags, but the mountain, apparently absolutely inaccessible, is the last point which you would turn for an outlet. A side gorge that sweeps up to the glaciers and snowy pyramids flashing upon you in the opposite direction is the route which you suppose your guide is going to take. So convinced was I that the path must go in that direction, that I took a shortcut, which I conceived would bring me again into the mule path at a point under the glaciers; but after scaling precipices and getting lost in a wood of firs in the valley, I was glad to rejoin my friend with the guide, and to clamber on in pure ignorance and wonder."

We are tempted to walk our own way when we have no other resource. But as Christians we have a higher resource than our mind. We have the resource of the lovingkindness of God, which can be ours every morning if we but seek it. We should never attempt to walk alone throughout the day and to chart our own course when we have the ability to tap the resources of Heaven in the morning and receive our marching orders for the day, marching orders that are always designed to lead to victory. How foolish it is to neglect to seek the Lord in the morning and have to walk without Him the rest of the day.

MORNING HYMN

Thou my everlasting portion,
More than friend or life to me;
All along my pilgrim journey,
Saviour, let me walk with Thee.

Vengeance

MORNING SCRIPTURE   1 Samuel 25:1-38
MORNING VERSE   1 Samuel 25:36
And Abigail came to Nabal; and, behold, he held a feast in his house, like the feast of a king and Nabal's heart was merry within him, for he was very drunken. wherefore she told him nothing, less or more, until the morning light.

One of the most obnoxious men in the Bible is Nabal. Nabal was a wealthy shepherd who had many flocks and servants. It appears that David and his men showed kindness to Nabal's servants and gave protection to them. Subsequently David's men needed provision and refreshment and he sent them to Nabal. But when David's men arrived at Carmel, Nabal lashed out at them, ridiculed them, and refused any help to them. The Bible describes Nabal as a churlish man "and evil in his doings." This simply means that he was hard to deal with, a difficult person to get along with. Not recognizing the anointing of God on David Nabal demanded, "Who is David? and who is the son of Jesse?" He ranked David among the common mavericks of the day. Nabal sent David's men away empty-handed. When the men returned to David and reported to him how offensively Nabal had acted and how unfriendly he had been, David's anger was piqued.

Four hundred of David's warriors were prepared to march against Nabal and retaliate for his unfriendly attitude. This would have engaged David in a sinful tirade against a sinful tyrant. Had it not been for the intervention of God through the actions of the quick-thinking wife of Nabal, David would undoubtedly have shed innocent blood that day. But Abigail, Nabal's wife, intercepted the irate David, brought gifts to him, and persuaded him not to take vengeance against her husband. She was God's messenger to God's man and David said to Abigail, "Blessed be the Lord God of Israel, which sent thee this day to meet me; and blessed be thy advice, and blessed be thou, which hast kept me this day from coming to shed blood, and from avenging myself with mine own hand." Nabal's attitude was unforgivable, but David's reaction was equally un-forgivable. He would heed Abigail's advice, the same advice Paul gave to the Roman believers when he said, "Dearly be-loved, avenge not yourselves, but rather give place unto [God's] wrath: for it is written, Vengeance is Mine; I will repay, saith the Lord" (Romans 12:19).

When Abigail returned to tell her husband what she had done, since he was filled with wine she wisely decided to tell him nothing *until the morning light* (1 Samuel 25:36). *In the morn-ing* (verse 37), when Nabal was sober, Abigail related to him what she had done to spare his life and the reputation of David. At that point the churlish man apparently had a stroke and ten days later the Lord took his life. Abigail's wisdom permitted God to return the wickedness of Nabal upon his own head and still preserve David from making a foolish mistake.

General Robert E. Lee was asked what he thought of one of his fellow officers in the Confederate Army. This officer had made many derogatory remarks about General Lee. Lee rated him as a fine officer and good soldier. Someone questioned, say-ing, "General, I guess you don't know what he's been saying about you." Lee responded, "I know, but I was asked my opin-ion of him, not his opinion of me!"

Although we may be slandered or maligned by others we are not at liberty to do anything but show the love of the Lord Jesus unto them. Perhaps today you have an antagonist spread-ing falsehood about you. Do not plan to avenge the wrong you have been done; give place to God's wrath instead and speak kindly of that antagonist. Then and then alone will a difficult situation bring glory to the name of God.

MORNING HYMN

Open my eyes, that I may see
Glimpses of truth Thou hast for me;
Place in my hands the wonderful key
That shall unclasp and set me free.
Silently now I wait for Thee,
Ready, my God, Thy will to see;
Open my eyes—illumine me,
Spirit divine!

Hospitality and Inhospitality

MORNING SCRIPTURE   Judges 19:1-30
MORNING VERSE   Judges 19:5
And it came to pass on the fourth day, when they arose early in he morning, that he rose up to depart: and the damsel's father said unto his son-in-law, Comfort thine heart with a morsel of bread, and afterward go your way.

In the family life of the ancient Near East, two important and contrasting features stand out in bold relief. They are the hospitality of the common folk and the inhospitality of those who are evil and cruel. The story of Judges 19 portrays both these features.

According to the historical account, a certain Levite who resided in the hill country of Ephraim took a concubine from Bethlehem-judah. Having proven unfaithful to him, the woman returned to her father's house in Bethlehem and there remained four months. After this separation the Levite decided to propose a reconciliation and thus traveled south to Bethlehem to speak with the woman and her father. Apparently the reconciliation was accomplished immediately for the father was quite happy to see his son-in-law.

The house of the Bethlehem father-in-law is a prime example of hospitality in the ancient Near East. Three days the son-in-law remained in the house and there "they did eat and drink." It was now time to leave. On the fourth day, *they arose early in the morning* in order to escape the punishing rays of the Palestinian sun (Judges 19:5). But the damsel's father invited his son-in-law to stay and have bread with him one more time. Soon the day had worn away and the invitation to tarry all night and wait for the morrow was given. Again the next day *he arose early in the morning* with the intent to leave, but the same thing happened (Judges 19:8). As the day wore on the man received a second invitation to tarry throughout the night, but this time he refused. With his wife he left Bethlehem and began to journey even though he knew he could not reach Mount Ephraim by nightfall.

Bypassing Jerusalem because the Jebusites lived there, the man chose to travel three miles further north to Gibeah where he anticipated a more hospitable reception. He found none and thus made preparations to spend the night in the street. Finally he and his wife were taken in by a former resident of Ephraim who now lived in Gibeah.

At this point the story begins to sound like Sodom and Gomorrah all over again. Base men, sons of Satan, encircled the house and began to beat on the door demanding that these men engage in a homosexual relationship with them. Perhaps taking his cue from Lot (cf. Genesis 19:1-11), unbelievably the master of the house offered his daughter and the Levite's concubine to the vicious mob in place of his house guest. This pacified the bisexual mob who abused the concubine all night long. When the Levite *rose up in the morning* and opened the doors of the house there he found the woman lying on the threshold (Judges 19:26-27).

Hospitality and inhospitality, both are seen here. What is it that causes one man to open his home in a gesture of hospitality and another man to beat down the door of a home to perform an act of homosexuality? What brings one man to do that which is delightful in the eyes of God and another to do that which is despicable in the eyes of God? Perhaps the answer is that we are made in the image of God and therefore have a desire to do good but have been marred by our own sin and have an innate bent toward evil. The Bethlehem father-in-law and the Ephraimite from Gibeah both sought to please others. The homosexual mob of Gibeah sought only to please themselves. Seeking one's own pleasure at the expense of all others arises out of a heart that is deceitful and desperately wicked (Jeremiah 17:9). There is no control over such a heart, only a cure found in the grace of salvation.

MORNING HYMN

> *Now incline me to repent,*
> *Let me now my sins lament;*
> *Now my foul revolt deplore,*
> *Weep, believe, and sin no more.*

Hidden Resources

MORNING SCRIPTURE   2 Samuel 23:1-17
MORNING VERSE   2 Samuel 23:4
And he shall be as the light of the morning, when the sun riseth, even a morning without clouds; as the tender grass springing out of the earth by clear shining after rain.

David had returned to his capital city, Jerusalem. All serious challenges to his authority were now behind him. He was about to die at age seventy, having ruled Judah for seven years and as king over all Israel for another thirty-three years.

Indeed David was a very remarkable man. He had great ability, great insight, great grace. As a soldier, he was a mighty man of valor. As a poet, he was the "sweet psalmist of Israel." He was decisive in politics and chivalrous in war. But he was as human as he was great. Perhaps it's that quality about David that makes the man so lovable to us. David had boundless love for Jehovah and an unshakable faith and loyalty to Him. While he frequently stumbled and fell, he always knew how to get ahold of God, ask forgiveness, and go on for God. He had a true hunger to know the will of God and do it.

Second Samuel 23:1 claims to record the last words of David. Although these are the last literary or poetic words, David's final dying words are not recorded until 1 Kings 2. David describes the kind of man God would have as king of Israel. "He that ruleth over men must be just" (2 Samuel 23:3). One who would be king, president, prime minister, or any leader can never assume he or she possesses the qualifications for these important tasks unless that person has a sense of justice that is more than human. Human justice views all men as created equal. Divine justice views all men as created equal before God, a God with whom all men have to do. This is why the next clause is so important. A godly leader is one "ruling in the fear of God."

When Jethro counseled Moses about organizing Israel he said, "Moreover thou shalt provide out of all the people able men, such as fear God, men of truth, hating covetousness; and place such over them to be rulers of thousands, and rulers of hundreds, rulers of fifties, and rulers of tens" (Exodus 18:21). As important as it is that a ruler be just, the capability to be just arises only out of a fear of God. God would have no one rule Israel who did not fear Him.

How can we draw upon the resource of the fear of God in order to be just to all men? We must depend upon our hidden resources. All nature depends on hidden resources. Rivers, deep and wide, have their sources in the snowcapped mountains. Great trees are only as strong as the part you cannot see, their root system. The entire earth draws upon the water and minerals under the ground, their hidden resources. A ruler in America, in Israel, anywhere in the world, will only be as great as his fear of God, and his fear of God will only be as deep as his hidden resources in God. This is why choosing a nation's leader must go beyond partisan politics, beyond basic morality, beyond simple decency.

David was keenly aware that he had not always exhibited the fear of God, the kind of fear that is pure, pristine, and clear. He describes the just man who fears God as one who "shall be as the *light of the morning,* when the sun riseth, *even a morning* without clouds" (2 Samuel 23:4). This kind of clearness and brightness comes only to a man who seeks the Lord, his hidden resource, early in the morning before he begins to make the decisions of his day. Let's pray that God will give us that kind of ruler.

MORNING HYMN
> *Take time to be holy,*
> *Speak oft with thy Lord;*
> *Abide in Him always*
> *And feed on His Word.*
> *Make friends of God's children,*
> *Help those who are weak*
> *Forgetting in nothing*
> *His blessing to seek.*

God's Providence

MORNING SCRIPTURE   1 Samuel 29
MORNING VERSE   1 Samuel 29:10
Wherefore now rise up early in the morning with thy master's servants that are come with thee: and as soon as ye be up early in the morning, and have light, depart.

W hen we live lives that are pleasing before the Lord, godly lives, righteous lives, we may always be assured that no matter where our steps take us, we have been led there by the Lord God Himself. Indeed, "The steps of a good man are ordered by the LORD" (Psalm 37:23).

By this time in his life the madness of King Saul had become so notable that he nearly destroyed himself and his nation as well. His hatred for David and his jealousy of this young Bethlehemite caused David to be resigned to a life of wandering. Once David learned that the Philistines were besieging the city of Keilah, he immediately hurried to rescue the city. Successful in his rescue, he drove off the enemy and scattered them, making this for a short time his headquarters (1 Samuel 23:1-6). However, whenever Saul learned of the whereabouts of David he was sure to be persistent in his pursuit of him and again David was forced to flee (1 Samuel 23:7-14). Although during his wanderings David attracted to his side six hundred soldiers in support of his cause, nevertheless these were days of hardship and grief for David. Finally he had to leave the kingdom entirely and seek refuge among his former enemies, the Philistines.

Although the enemy clearly remembered that David slew the giant Goliath, now he was an enemy of Israel's king and so the Philistines made an unlikely alliance with David and his men. With the consent of Achish, king of Gath, David made his headquarters at Ziklag for more than a year (1 Samuel 27:1-7). Because he supported the Philistine king in raids on the tribes to the south of the wilderness of Shur (1 Samuel 27:8-12), David gained the respect and friendship of Achish. Things were fine as long as the Philistines were fighting someone other than the Israelites. But that situation was about to change.

The Philistine armies assembled at Aphek to encounter the Israelites in Jezreel. David was now in a desperately ticklish situation. He was with the armies of the Philistines, arrayed in preparation for battle against his own people, Israel. What would he do? How would God get him out of this jam?

David didn't have to wait long for a resolution to the problem. The princes of the Philistines began to wonder whether or not they could trust David fighting against his own people. If he were to win the favor of King Saul again, what better way than to kill the Philistines. Therefore Achish commanded, "Wherefore now *rise up early in the morning* with thy master's servants that are come with thee: and as soon as ye be *up early in the morning*, and have light, depart" (1 Samuel 29:10). Once again, through the suspicions of the Philistines, God had spared David from fighting against his own people.

Rowland V. Bingham, founder of the Sudan Interior Mission, was once seriously injured in a terrible automobile accident. Rushed to the hospital in critical condition, he did not regain consciousness until the next day. When he asked the nurse what he was doing there, she replied, "Don't try to talk now, just rest. You have been in an accident." "Accident? Accident?" exclaimed Dr. Bingham. "There are no accidents in the life of the Christian. This is just an incident in God's perfect leading." Our attitude toward the Lord's leading our steps ought to be the same. When we live righteously before Him, free from known sin, there are no accidents in our lives, only incidents in His perfect leading. Let Him lead you today.

MORNING HYMN

In shady, green pastures, so rich and so sweet,
God leads His dear children along,
Where the water's cool flow bathes the weary one's feet,
God leads His dear children along.
Some thru the waters, some thru the flood,
Some thru the fire, but all thru the blood;
Some thru great sorrow, but God gives a song,
In the night season and all the day long.

Morning Praise

MORNING SCRIPTURE   Psalm 113:1-9
MORNING VERSE   Psalm 113:3
From the rising of the sun unto the going down of the same the LORD's *name is to be praised.*

L ike the two psalms preceding it this one is without title. Some commentators have ascribed it to Samuel others to David. However the authorship is unknown. Whoever the author was, in his best journalistic style he answers the five key questions that any young reporter would ask when writing a story: he answers the five W's: who, what, when, where, and why. Let's notice what has excited this young reporter to write in such a way.

Who. To whom does the writer speak? To all of us. Anyone who reads this psalm is included in the "ye" of verse 1, most specifically, "O ye servants of the LORD." More than anyone else, the servants of the Lord ought to be involved in the exalted activity of praising God. Each of us who claims to serve the Lord must publicly discharge our responsibility We are best acquainted with the reasons for praising Him and we are also the best instruments to declare His praise.

What. The responsibility of the servants of the Lord is simply, "Praise ye the LORD ...praise the name of the LORD." The repetition of this phrase in a single verse is not without significance. You would think that we who have been saved by His grace would automatically and consistently praise His name. However this is not the case, for we are frequently slow in praising God for His blessings. Therefore the psalmist finds it necessary to stimulate us, to cajole us, and the repetition of the stimulus calls us to perseverance in sounding forth the praises of God.

When. To indicate when the servants of the Lord are to be engaged in praising the Lord the psalmist uses an expression which is more characteristic of the old Greek poets than of the Hebrew prophets. He says, "*From the rising of the sun* unto the going down of the same the LORD's name is to be praised" (Psalm 113:3). This poetic expression indicates that there is never a time of the day, never a waking hour, never an inappropriate moment, when the servant of the Lord cannot praise His name. We are to begin His praise at the very rising of the sun, early in the morning, and to continue that praise until sunset. Praising the name of the Lord is a daylong, lifelong privilege.

Where. If we are to praise the Lord from the rising of the sun until the going down of the same, where is it we shall engage in this exalted activity? Since "the LORD is high above all nations, and His glory above heaven," and yet He "humbleth himself to behold the things that are in heaven, and in the earth," it is incumbent upon us to see that His name is praised wherever His presence is known. Therefore we are to praise His name in the highest heavens and the lowest earth. Just as there is not a waking hour that is inappropriate to praise His name, there is not the slightest place on earth that is inappropriate to the praising of His name. As servants of the Lord, we are to praise Him continually, wherever we find ourselves.

Why. The reasons for praising the Lord are manifold. He is high above all nations, and His glory above the heavens. Still he humbleth Himself to observe our affairs on earth. He raiseth the poor out of the dust and the needy out of the dunghill. He makes princes out of paupers and makes the barren woman a homemaker and the mother of children.

Today would be a good day for us to make a praise list. Just as we have a prayer list, Christians ought to have a praise list, a list of reasons for praising the Lord. Begin with His love for you, His death for you, and His salvation of you, and keep listing things for which to praise the Lord from morning to night. Don't be surprised if you have to make a second list for we have much for which to praise the Lord. A praise list—it's an idea worth consideration.

MORNING HYMN

> *O for a thousand tongues to sing*
> *My great Redeemer's praise,*
> *The glories of my God and King,*
> *The triumphs of His grace.*

He Is Alive

MORNING SCRIPTURE   Mark 16:1-20
MORNING VERSE   Mark 16:9

Now when Jesus was risen early the first day of the week, He appeared first to Mary Magdalene, out of whom He had cast seven devils.

Perhaps the most astounding event ever to take place early in the morning occurred on the first Easter morning. God is in the habit of doing things early in the morning but on this particular morning He did something very special. He raised Jesus Christ from the dead and the mighty power of God was proved by the post-resurrection appearances of our Lord.

In Mark 16 three such appearances of the risen Saviour are recorded. Verse 14 indicates that "He appeared unto the eleven as they sat at meat." The disciples had assembled themselves, except Thomas, and were not given to believing the reports that Jesus was alive. Suddenly He appeared in their midst, the doors of the room being shut, and they perceived Him to be a spirit. But He called unto them to feel His body, He showed them the wounds in His hands, His feet, and His side. As some still doubted, He ate food before them all. He rebuked them for their lack of faith. But He also commissioned them to "Go ye into all the world, and preach the gospel to every creature" (verse 15). This was the last of His appearances on that great resurrection day.

Prior to this occasion, however, He appeared to two individuals walking on the road to Emmaus. Although only briefly mentioned by Mark, the interesting narrative given by Luke tells us that Cleopas and another had left the city after visiting the sepulcher and were on their way to the village of Emmaus, some seven miles from Jerusalem. As they were engaged in conversation, Jesus Himself joined them. They invited Him to accompany them to the home of Cleopas; they did not recognize Him as the risen Lord. Suddenly, "And beginning at Moses and all the prophets, he expounded unto them in all the scriptures the things concerning himself" (Luke 24:27). Still, when they reported to the others that they had met the risen Lord, the disciples found that difficult to believe.

But to whom was the first postresurrection appearance made? Did Jesus first appear to Peter, the principal preacher of Christianity in the first century? Did He appear to John, the beloved disciple, the disciple whom Jesus loved? No, He appeared to one whose devotion to Him could not be excelled. He appeared to one whose dedication to Him could not be surpassed. He appeared first to one who was an unlikely candidate for such an honor. Mark 16:9 says, "Now when Jesus was risen early the first day of the week He appeared first to Mary Magdalene, out of whom He had cast seven devils." Yes, Mary Magdalene would be the first one to see the risen Lord even though she was not an apostle nor would she ever be used of God to write a single line of Scripture. Her only qualification for this high honor was her deep and abiding affection for her Lord.

The Gospel of Luke records that when Jesus was preaching in every city and village, the twelve disciples being with Him, a company of women followed them. This occurred out of sheer gratitude for what the Lord had done in their behalf. One of them was Mary called Magdalene, out of whom Jesus cast seven devils. From the moment of her exorcism by the Lord Jesus, Mary followed her Master and the disciple band and ministered unto Him, as did the other women, of their substance (Luke 8:1-3). This unremitting devotion was the quality found by the Lord to be the most rewardable of all.

It is not as important what we bring to the service of the Lord as it is how much we love the Lord we serve. Mary would never be used as the disciples would; she would never be recorded as one of the great leaders of the first century Church. Still, Jesus first appeared to Mary Magdalene after His resurrection because she, in absolute devotion to her Master, was keeping a vigil outside the tomb after she had reported to Peter and John that Jesus of Nazareth was risen. Oh that our devotion to the Lord would parallel that of this simple woman. How much we love Him is far more important than how much we serve Him

MORNING HYMN

> *Risen for me, risen for me,*
> *Up from the grave He has risen for me;*
> *Now evermore from death's sting I am free,*
> *All because Jesus has risen for me.*

Pride

MORNING SCRIPTURE   2 Samuel 24:1-25
MORNING VERSE   2 Samuel 24:11
*For when David was up in the morning, the word of the Lord
came unto the prophet Gad, David's seer.*

H ave you ever noticed that you make your greatest mistakes immediately after your greatest victories? Why is
that? The answer is likely pride. The Bible frequently
warns us about the penalty of pride. Proverbs 16:18 says, "Pride
goeth before destruction and an haughty spirit before a fall."
The pages of the Holy Scriptures are filled with people who
have met their defeat, not because of their inferiority, but because of their haughty and arrogant spirit.

A graphic illustration of the penalty of pride is seen in the
life of King David. A man after God's own heart, David early
won favor with Jehovah for his faithfulness and purity of life.
He rose above the usurpation of his throne by two of his sons.
He lived down the shame of his sin with Bathsheba. Now he
had come to the end of his life, a valiant warrior and a victor.

Following the catalog of David's mighty men is the statement, "And again the anger of the LORD was kindled against
Israel, and he moved David against them to say, Go, number
Israel and Judah" (2 Samuel 24:1). The wrath of God was upon
His people at this time not so much for a specific offense as for
the general deterioration of their faithfulness to Him. First
Chronicles 21:1 indicates that it was Satan who incited David to
take this census. Although the penalty for this sin affected all
people, David accepted it as the result of his own personal sin.
Why? Because the numbering of the people was done in pride,
for the purpose of self-glory, and pride always pays a penalty.

Immediately after David learned the strength of his army,
he recognized the basis for his need to know their number. "And
David said unto the LORD, I have sinned greatly in that I have
done ...for I have done very foolishly." As soon as David was
up in the morning (2 Samuel 24:11), God offered three potential
punishments for this pride. David's options were not good: the

people could endure seven years of famine; David could flee three months from his enemies; Israel could experience three days of the worst pestilence they had ever seen. David preferred to receive punishment from God rather than from his enemies. Thus the Lord sent a pestilence upon Israel in the morning. Because of Israel's continued sin and David's pride, seventy thousand men died during the next three days in Israel.

There is an old fable about two ducks and a frog that played together in a small pond. Each summer, when the days got long and hot, the pond shrank to a small puddle and the ducks and frog were forced to move. The ducks could fly to another place, but not the frog. As the fable goes, the frog finally suggested that the ducks put a stick in their bills so he could cling to it with his mouth and thus fly away with them. The frog was very proud of his brilliant idea. As the ducks took off for a nearby lake, the stick between their bills and the frog clinging tightly, they passed over a farmer who seeing this strange sight questioned, "Well, isn't that a clever stunt! I wonder who thought of it?" Swelling with pride, the frog said, "I did!" and with that he lost his grip and went crashing to the ground. His own pride had done him in.

Let us beware of our pride today, for it may lead to the same kind of painful end that the frog experienced. Even worse, it may lead to pain inflicted upon others, as was experienced in the life of David. Remember, "Pride goeth before destruction" (Proverbs 16:18).

MORNING HYMN
> *Lord Jesus, look down from Thy throne in the skies*
> *And help me to make a complete sacrifice.*
> *I give up myself and whatever I know—*
> *Now wash me and I shall be whiter than snow*

Relying on God

MORNING SCRIPTURE   Psalm 127:1-5
MORNING VERSE   Psalm 127:2
It is vain for you to rise up early, to sit up late, to eat the bread of sorrows: for so He giveth His beloved sleep.

T he theme of this delightful little psalm is the folly of human effort apart from God. Anything we attempt in life is doomed to failure unless we rely on the power of God. The psalmist shows us this is true in four aspects of human life: social (verse 1a); civic (verse 1b); business (verse 2); and domestic (verses 3-5). In each of these there is an unmistakable emphasis on the necessity for reliance an God.

"Except the Lord build the house, they labour in vain that build it." Regardless if it is a private dwelling or the house of God, it is useless to undertake building unless we seek the prosperity of God. The psalmist does not say that unless the Lord consents that the house should be built, he says unless the Lord builds the house. We supply the materials; He does the work in our social lives.

"Except the Lord keep the city, the watchman waketh but in vain." Turning from social to civic life, the psalmist knows the unseen watchman of every city is Jehovah Himself. The constant vigilance of a sentinel is without reward if he watches alone. It does little good for us to stand watch unless the Lord stands with us. Not to set a watch when the enemy is at hand is foolish, but to set a watch in our own strength is just as foolish.

"It is vain for you to *rise up early*, to sit up late, to eat the bread of sorrows." Here the psalmist does not counsel us against rising early. His intent is to show us that nothing is accomplished by rising early or staying up late if all we do is fret about our problems. Here too we must have absolute dependence upon God.

Finally, the psalmist turns his attention to reliance on God in domestic matters. He begins with a statement about children which is diametrically opposed to the philosophy of the world today. In a day in which children are frequently viewed as a bother, an infringement on personal freedom, and are therefore aborted before they are born, the psalmist counters, "Lo, children are an heritage of the Lord." Children come to us from God and are another means of building a house. In fact, in the Hebrew, the word for son (*ben*) and daughter (*bath*) both come from the same root word for house (*beth*). Although building a house is akin to building sons and daughters, building sons and daughters is more important than building a house around them.

A preacher once was entertained by a couple who had two teenage boys. When he entered the house he noticed immediately a sense of warmth. He also noticed that the living room carpet was very tattered. Before he left, the mother related that one day several boys from the neighborhood were having a good time in her living room. Perhaps they were being a little too rough and she asked them to play elsewhere. They responded, "But where will we go?" Nodding to one of them she asked, "How about your place?" "Not a chance," replied the boy. "We're not allowed to invite kids into our house." Others questioned gave similar replies. The mother soon sensed that her home was the only one where the boys felt free to come and have fun. From then on they were always welcome.

While the mother did not allow the children to be disrespectful to her property, she nonetheless recognized that the rug was only property, but that children were an heritage from the Lord. She knew if she were to raise a family she would have to show a lot of love and rely on the Lord.

To whatever endeavor God calls you today, whether it be social, civic, business, or domestic, reliance on Him is a prerequisite to success. You cannot build a house fruitfully without the labor of God. You cannot watch a city successfully without the protection of God. You cannot engage in business tirelessly without the strength of God. You cannot raise children lovingly without the wisdom of God. All human activity is but folly unless you rely upon God for success. Ask Him to make you successful today.

MORNING HYMN

> *If God build not the house, and lay*
> *The groundwork sure—whoever build,*
> *It cannot stand one stormy day.*
> *If God be not the city's shield,*
> *If He be not their bars and wall,*
> *In vain is watchtower; men, and all.*

Jesus First

MORNING SCRIPTURE   Revelation 22.1-21
MORNING VERSE   Revelation 22.16
I Jesus have sent mine angel to testify unto you these things in the churches. I am the root and the offspring of David, and the bright and morning star.

J ust as Genesis, the first book of the Bible, is a book of beginnings, Revelation, the last book of the Bible, is a book of new beginnings. Before these new beginnings can occur, however, a series of endings must transpire. Thus the book of Revelation represents numerous "finals" in the Word of God.

Genesis 3:9 is God's initial call to man: "And the LORD God called unto Adam, and said unto him, Where art thou?" Revelation 22:17 is God's final call to man: "And the Spirit and the bride say, come. And let him that heareth say, Come. And let him that is athirst come. And whosoever will, let him take the water of life freely." Somewhere between Genesis 3:9 and Revelation 22:17 everyone who would enjoy eternity in Heaven with Christ must answer one of God's calls. Perhaps you have answered Jesus' call in Matthew 11:28, "Come unto Me, all ye that labour and are heavy laden, and I will give you rest." Or maybe it was the call of Christ in John 4:14, "But whosoever drinketh of the water that I shall give him shall never thirst; but the water that I shall give him shall be in him a well of water springing up into everlasting life." But if you have not responded to the call of Christ, if you have never received Jesus Christ as your Saviour, you must respond to His call in order to receive eternal life.

Once we have responded positively to the Lord's call to salvation, we have a whole new outlook on the future. Our destiny is brighter. Our lives are sunnier. The birds' songs are sweeter. We look forward to serving Jesus every day and anticipate the day we shall live with Him in glory.

Just before God's final call in Revelation 22:17, Jesus verifies that He is indeed the one to whom we are called in salvation. He says, "I am the root and the offspring of David, and the *bright and morning star*" (Revelation 22:16). These titles are applied to Him elsewhere in Scripture (cf. Isaiah 11:1; Numbers 24:17), but nowhere do they take on more meaning than just prior to the final call in the Bible. When we come to God in salvation, we come to the offspring of David. When we leave the darkness of sin, we enter the light of the Bright and Morning Star. It is the shining face of Jesus, the one who died for us, that we will first want to see when we enter the brightness of Heaven. After all, being with our Saviour is what makes Heaven heavenly.

When Fanny Crosby, the hymn writer who wrote more than eight thousand gospel songs even though she was blinded at the age of six weeks, was pitied by a friend because she could not see, Miss Crosby replied, "Do you know that if at birth I had been able to make one petition, it would have been that I would have been born blind?" The friend was puzzled by this answer and asked her for further explanation. "Because when I get to Heaven, the first face that shall ever gladden my sight will be that of my Saviour!" We too will want to see our Saviour first of all.

There is a story about Cyrus, the founder of the Persian Empire, who once captured a prince and his entire family. When they came before the monarch, Cyrus asked the prisoner, "What will you give me if I release you?" The prince replied, "The half of my wealth." "And if I release your children?" Again the prince replied, "Everything I possess." Finally Cyrus said, "And what will you give me if I will release your wife?" The prince replied, "Your Majesty, I will give myself." So moved was Cyrus by the devotion of this young prince that he freed him and his entire family. As the prince, his wife, and children returned to their home, the prince said to his wife, "Wasn't Cyrus a handsome man!" With a tender look of love in her eyes, the wife said to her husband, "I did not notice. I could only keep my eyes on you—the one who was willing to give himself for me."

Morning by morning we arise to give praise to the one who saved us. Day by day we serve the one who saved us. Evening by evening we rejoice in the one who saved us. Let's concentrate today on loving the Lord Jesus and adoring no other face than the one who loved us so much that He died for us (John 3:16).

MORNING HYMN
> *All hail the pow'r of Jesus' name!*
> *Let angels prostrate fall;*
> *Bring forth the royal diadem,*
> *And crown Him Lord of all.*

Standing Tall

MORNING SCRIPTURE   Job 1:1-22
MORNING VERSE   Job 1:5
And it was so, when the days of their feasting were gone about, that Job sent and sanctified them, and rose up early in the morning, and offered burnt offerings according to the number of them all: for Job said, It may be that my sons have sinned, and cursed God in their hearts. Thus did Job continually.

The ability to meet affliction with an uncompromising endurance and an unflinching respect for God is one of the marks of true Christian character Certainly Job is the classic example of a man who met affliction in such a way.

The author begins the book of Job by describing a beautiful pastoral scene in which Job, a respected and honored oriental sheik or prince, was residing in the land of Uz. Job was a man of extreme wealth possessing a flock of seven thousand sheep, three thousand camels, large tracts of land, and an affectionate family of seven sons and three daughters.

But more than this, Job was a man of extreme piety. The first verse of the book describes him as "perfect and upright, and one that feared God, and eschewed evil." So concerned was this man about keeping himself and his family right before his God that he *"rose up early in the morning,* and offered burnt offerings according to the number of them all; for Job said, It may be that my sons have sinned, and cursed God in their hearts. Thus did Job continually" (Job 1:5). Day after day he met God early, bringing sacrifices to the Almighty in the event that he or any of his family had secretly sinned against God.

The rest of this chapter's verses, comprising scene two in the first act of Job's life, read like a horror story. Here Satan entered this beautiful country scene and disrupted the simple pastoral life of Job and his family. Notice these features of scene two.

1. *Satan's report* (verse 6). The day came when the sons of God, presumably the angels, were to bring a report of their activities to Jehovah. Satan also came among them.

2. *Satan's activity* (verse 7). When Jehovah asked Satan why

he had come and from where he had come, Lucifer answered the Lord, "From going to and fro in the earth, and from walking up and down in it." Satan's activity was a never-ending search for opportunities to disrupt the program of God.

3. *Satan's problem* (verse 8). It was Jehovah who suggested to Satan, "Hast thou considered My servant Job?" Here Satan would encounter a man who was perfect and upright, one who hated every kind of evil that Satan had placed in his path.

4. *Satan's accusation* (verses 10-11). The devil had a ready answer for why Job had remained upright. God had put a hedge around him so that everything Job did prospered. Surely if God would remove that hedge, Satan reasoned, Job certainly would curse God to His face.

5. *Satan's restriction* (verse 12). Jehovah permitted Lucifer to touch all that Job possessed but placed one restriction upon him, "Only upon himself put not forth thine hand." Although God does not always make this temporal restriction with regard to us today, he certainly makes it an eternal restriction.

6. *Satan's attacks* (verses 13-19). The devil came to menace Job. Like waves of enemy soldiers the reports kept coming to Job until he learned that he had lost all.

7. *Satan's failure* (verses 20-22). Job arose and reacted with characteristic remorse. And yet, rather than sin and foolishly charge God, Job stood tall and simply stated, "Naked came I out of my mother's womb, and naked shall I return thither: the LORD gave and the LORD hath taken away; blessed be the name of the LORD (Job 1:21).

Do not be discouraged when you face the attacks of the wicked one. These attacks are only temporal and our loving God will have the final word. You may not always understand the ways of God, but you must always trust them, as did Job.

MORNING HYMN

> *Why should I feel discouraged,*
> *Why should the shadows come,*
> *Why should my heart be lonely*
> *And long for Heav'n and home,*
> *When Jesus is my portion?*
> *My constant Friend is He;*
> *His eye is on the sparrow,*
> *And I know He watches me*

Ingredients for Service

MORNING SCRIPTURE   Exodus 34:1-35
MORNING VERSE   Exodus 34:2
And be ready in the morning, and come up in the morning unto mount Sinai and present thyself there to Me in the top of the mount.

T he man who bows the lowest in the presence of God stands the straightest in the presence of sin. If this truth was known by anyone in the Old Testament, it was known by Moses. Time after time he had to stand straight and tall in the face of Israel's sin. Once even while Moses was communing with God on the top of Sinai, Israel was brewing a pot of sin. Upon his descent from the mount, viewing the golden calf and licentious behavior of Israel, Moses' righteous indignation caused him to cast the tables of God's Law to the ground, crushing them to pieces (Exodus 32:19). The people were rebuked for their sin, three thousand men were capitally punished, Moses interceded for the lives of the rest, and the golden calf crisis was over.

But there would be more sin and the tables of stone had to be replaced. Thus the Lord issued Moses another summons to Sinai with these instructions: "And be ready *in the morning,* and come up *in the morning* unto mount Sinai, and present thyself there to Me in the top of the mount" (Exodus 34:2). Note the words, "be ready," "come up," and "present thyself." Moses' renewed call to service contained these three essential ingredients found in every call to service God issues.

Be ready. The man God uses is the man who is ready, willing, and able to be used. If we are not ready, God will bypass us for someone who is, and we will miss the blessing that could have been ours. The Apostle Paul was a man who was ready. In Romans 1:15 he was "ready to preach the gospel to you that are at Rome also." With Paul preaching was a passion: "For I am ready not to be bound only, but also to die at Jerusalem for the name of the Lord Jesus" (Acts 21:13). After a long life of service to his Lord, Paul exclaimed, "For I am now ready to be offered, and the time of my departure is at hand. I have fought a good

209

fight, I have finished my course, I have kept the faith" (2 Timothy 4:6-7). Paul was ready to preach, ready to suffer, even ready to die in the service of the Lord.

Come up. We cannot be of service to God until we first come to Him in salvation. But Jehovah's call to Moses was not to salvation but to communion and service. Once the Lord has called us to be saved, He then calls us to "come and dine" (John 21:12). In other words, as Moses, we are called to fellowship with the Lord. We "come up" to the Lord God in prayer. Like salvation, prayer and communion with God precede service (Ephesians 6:18-20).

Present thyself. The final ingredient in preparing for service to God and standing in the face of sin is to present ourselves to Him. Paul begged the Roman believers to "present your bodies a living sacrifice, holy, acceptable unto God, which is your reasonable service" (Romans 12:1). Being ready to serve God is necessary. Coming up to God in prayer is likewise necessary in preparing for useful service. But unless we are willing to present ourselves to God—body, mind, and soul—as Moses did, there is little chance that He will use us or that we will successfully stand straight and tall in the presence of sin.

When the call of God came, Moses prepared a second pair of stone tablets for the law of God and *"rose up early in the morning,* and went up unto Mount Sinai, as the Lᴏʀᴅ had commanded him" (Exodus 34:4). Moses was ready for service, early in the morning, for he knew that there was a lot of sin yet to be dealt with in the camp of Israel. Moses must stand straight and tall in the presence of that sin, as each believer must. Are you ready to rise early each morning and come to God in prayer, presenting yourself in service to Him? Your day will go much better if you are.

MORNING HYMN

> *Stand up, stand up for Jesus,*
> *Ye soldiers of the cross;*
> *Lift high His royal banner,*
> *It must not suffer loss:*
> *From vict'ry unto vict'ry*
> *His army shall He lead,*
> *Till ev'ry foe is vanquished,*
> *And Christ is Lord indeed*

The Hidden Hammer

MORNING SCRIPTURE   Job 7:1-21
MORNING VERSE   Job 7:21
And why dost thou not pardon my transgression, and take away mine iniquity? for now shall I sleep in the dust; and thou shalt seek me in the morning, but I shall not be.

The bottom had fallen out of Job's life. All his possessions had been destroyed. His family had been slaughtered, and any hope for a posterity was gone. God had delivered Job into Satan's hand. Those associated with Job could not understand why this had happened. Even his wife counseled him to "curse God and die" (Job 2:9). But Job was fully convinced that if God had permitted this evil to come to him the evil would ultimately turn to good.

Job's friend Eliphaz expressed surprise that Job, who in the past comforted others, was now giving way to sorrow. His friend wrongly judged that if Job had nothing to be ashamed of, he had no reason to be sorrowful. Theologically he understood misfortune always to be the result of sin. Therefore there was no other explanation than that Job had sinned and the route of escape was not a bitter complaint but a bold confession of sin to receive the fruit of blessing. Understandably Job was offended at the speech of his friend. Eliphaz had magnified Job's complaint and minimized his condition. Just think of it. Life had collapsed around him and Job could think of no specific cause for that. He knew Eliphaz was wrong in his assessment of the situation.

In chapter 7 Job is philosophical about the brevity of life. He knows that the days of man upon the earth are numbered. He likens them to the cloud that is consumed and vanishes away. Since life is so brief and his life is now so filled with anguish, why does Jehovah even bother with Job? Why does He reveal Himself to Job every morning and try him every moment (Job 7:18)? In his condition, life is worth less than death and Job desires that "thou shalt seek me in the morning, but I shall not be" (Job 7:21). The blows that God permitted Satan to land on Job appear to have been merciless. His life had been upright and just. How could God allow this to happen?

Samuel Chadwick relates that when he was a boy he often went to the local blacksmith shop to watch the smithy work. He remembers how the smith would take a large piece of iron and place it in the fire with tongs and then work the bellows to make it white-hot. Then after removing the piece of iron from the fire and laying it upon the anvil, he would take a small hammer and begin to tap on the iron. No sooner would the smith tap the iron with the small hammer than a big man on the other side of the anvil would come crashing down hard with a large sledge hammer, hitting the iron on the exact same spot that the blacksmith had just tapped. Inquisitively, Chadwick once commented to the blacksmith, "You don't do much good with that little hammer, do you?" The gentle blacksmith laughed and replied, "No, my boy, but I show that big fellow where to place the blow."

When the bottom fell out of Job's life and his friends came to comfort him, none of them was aware of all that had transpired in Heaven before these calamities began. None of them knew that God had given Satan permission to afflict Job. They were totally unaware that while Satan was pounding away at Job with his unholy sledge hammer, each blow was being carefully guided by a loving Heavenly Father. God would show Satan where he could deliver his blows on Job, just like the blacksmith defined for his large friend where he could hit the iron with his sledge hammer.

If you are today experiencing unjust criticism, undue persecution, or unreturned love, please remember that as a child of God Satan can never afflict you beyond that which God, your loving Heavenly Father, gives him permission to do. God is still in control and though friends may unrighteously condemn us, as long as we live a life clean before Him, we need not be concerned about what Satan can do to us.

MORNING HYMN

Day by day and with each passing moment,
Strength I find to meet my trials here;
Trusting in my Father's wise bestowment,
I've no cause for worry or for fear,
He whose heart is kind beyond all measure
Gives unto each day what He deems best,
Lovingly, its part of pain and pleasure,
Mingling toil with peace and rest.

Early in the Morning

Early in the morning
    I rise to meet the Lord,
He makes His presence known to me
    Through the pages of His Word.

For when I meet Him early
    At the dawning of the day,
The hours go more smoothly
    Whatever comes my way.

But if I fail to meet Him
    And rush to other things,
I face the kind of failures
    That a day without Him brings.

So here's a little secret
    To make your day go right,
Meet God early in the morning
    And praise Him every night.

KROLL